THE
COURAGE
TO BELIEVE

THE COURAGE TO BELIEVE

CRAIG MORTON
AND
ROBERT BURGER

Prentice-Hall, Inc., Englewood Cliffs, New Jersey

Biblical quotes are from several different translations—
the preference of the subjects.

The author wishes to express appreciation for permission to quote from the following:
"Unreflecting Egoism" by Robert Coles © 1979,
The New Yorker Magazine, Inc.;
The Art of Loving by Erich Fromm, Harper & Row, 1956;
Article by Doris Lessing from *The New York Times Book Review* © 1980;
Second Wind © 1979 by William F. Russell;
Grapes of Wrath © 1939 by John Steinbeck;
Terry Bradshaw: Man of Steel by Terry Bradshaw with Dave Diles,
copyright © 1979 by The Zondervan Corporation.

The Courage to Believe by
Craig Morton and Robert Burger
Copyright © 1981 by
Craig Morton and Robert Burger

Printed in the United States of America
Prentice-Hall International, Inc., London
Prentice-Hall of Australia, Pty. Ltd., Sydney
Prentice-Hall of Canada, Ltd., Toronto
Prentice-Hall of India Private Ltd., New Delhi
Prentice-Hall of Japan, Inc., Tokyo
Prentice-Hall of Southeast Asia Pte. Ltd., Singapore
Whitehall Books Limited, Wellington, New Zealand
10 9 8 7 6 5 4

Library of Congress Cataloging in Publication Data
Morton, Craig.
    The courage to believe.
    1. Athletes—Biography.   2. Religion and
sports.   I. Burger, Robert E., joint author.
    II. Title.
    GV697.A1M597   796'.092'2 [B]   81-47

ISBN 0-13-184416-4

To all those who so graciously and beautifully shared their lives with me, and to my son Michael, with hopes that he too will have the courage to share his beliefs.

A most rewarding aspect of the preparation of this book has been the unquestioning cooperation of the athletes whose experiences are related here; their families; their teams. Our thanks to them all, and especially to Minetta Miller of Denver.

FOREWORD

Like millions of other Americans, I grew up in the presence of religion without really being touched by it. I was well into my thirties before I came to understand that there is a meaning in life and a purpose that can enrich our lives. I was once afraid to use words like "meaning" and "purpose" because I thought they were too fancy. I believed in tangible things like hitting a baseball or owning a car. So now, as I approach this book—in which I hope to share the beliefs that have enriched *my* life— my only fear is that you too will back away from this "born-again Christian" just because of the words.

This book is addressed primarily to those who are in the same boat I was in in my youth and early adulthood. I know them all too well. Most of them live respectable, even generous lives—as I thought I did. They may go through the usual ups and downs of growing up and earning a living, but they eventually settle down, raise families, establish careers, or even become leaders in their communities. Whether they have religious beliefs or not doesn't seem to make much difference. If they suffer some serious crisis or personal tragedy, they may turn to religon for help, but otherwise it really doesn't touch them.

It seems to me that the people I am describing avoid becoming involved with Christianity for one simple reason: they think it's an extra burden. They think of beliefs in terms of what those beliefs demand of them, challenge them to do, restrict them from doing. They don't need religion, they think, because they don't need any more burdens. *They are afraid to believe.*

If there is only one thing I can get across to you in this book, I hope it is this: a belief in Christ will enrich you, not limit you; it will gladden you, not depress you; it will give you joy, not guilt. It will not hold you back, but give you the fullness of life.

Because so many people carry around a view of Christians as gloomy people, believers in magic or worse, out of touch with modern thinking, they shudder at the mention of the Bible or the Lord. I see people screw up their faces when I tell them I'm a born-again Christian, because they think that's some kind of a reformed, pious do-gooder. We live in such a skeptical age that the very word "do-gooder" is a put-down. And it bothers me when generous, fair-minded people, many of them old friends, cannot step across that border of disbelief and skepticism that once separated me from what I now experience in Christianity. They stop at the words alone—words like "born again."

So I will confess at the start to a little deception. In order to capture your attention long enough to cross that barrier of words, I have chosen ten people—besides myself—whose sports' backgrounds are interesting enough to illustrate various aspects of my point of view. Each of these ten has influenced me; each has made a striking point with his life, in my opinion. I hope you will find their stories interesting enough as *sports* stories, and in the process see the Christian story that is inextricably woven into their lives. That's my little deception.

I could have chosen any number of outstanding athletes, such as Jerry Lucas or Don Sutton or Randy Gradishar. I could have broadened the scope of religious beliefs by including such Jewish stars as Hank Greenberg or Sandy Koufax, or such Muslims as Muhammad Ali or Kareem Abdul-Jabbar. I could have given due credit to women by featuring Margaret Court or Jo Jo Starbuck. I tried, instead, to concentrate on what is closest to me—Christian athletes in three very demanding sports situations: football, track, and coaching. Four of my subjects are professional football players, three are football coaches, and three are runners from the mile to the marathon. They differ in age, in national prominence, and in lifestyle. Most important, each has a unique way of showing what it means to *believe*.

"I am a part of all that I have met," wrote Alfred Lord Tennyson. It is my hope that through this book each of these men, and what he stands for, may be a part of you.

CONTENTS

ONE

THE IMPOSSIBLE COMEBACK

CRAIG MORTON

One bleak fall afternoon in 1979, a man named Bob Peck sat in a wheelchair in the tunnel at the south end of Mile High Stadium in Denver and watched the team he loved get ready to receive another kickoff amid a growing snarl of boos. When the Denver Broncos were down 20–10 at the half, there was still hope. But now the Seattle Seahawks, in the opening six minutes of the third quarter, struck suddenly for two more touchdowns. The "Orange Crush," Denver's proud defense for several seasons, seemed unable to contain Seattle's exuberant young quarterback, Jim Zorn. I sat on the bench, hanging my head.

Bob had been the publicity director for our team for a decade—long before I joined them. He had lived through the growing pains of the Broncos under John Ralston and had

tasted the glory days when Red Miller guided us to the Super
Bowl. Even the following season, 1978, had its moments of
triumph, until Terry Bradshaw and the Pittsburgh Steelers
overpowered us in the AFC championship. If anybody during
those years could be credited with arousing the spirit of the
Denver faithful on Sunday afternoons, it was Bob Peck.

Then, out of the blue, Bob was struck down. The doctors
said it was one of those things that can hit any time, for no
apparent reason—a brain tumor. He was confined to the
hospital as the 1979 season opened. Now, during our fourth
game, a sort of homecoming called "Orange Sunday," he was
suffering a different kind of pain as our fans took out their
anger on the orange jerseys on the field. The scoreboard read
34–10.

After the Seattle kickoff I had my first chance to get the
seat of my pants off the bench. I called a quick screen at about
our thirty-five and hit Rick Upchurch for seventeen yards.
This had been my predictable role so far—to come in when
Norris Weese failed to put points on the board, and to try to
get the offense moving again. I had been watching Seattle's
man-to-man coverage and thought I could beat it. I found
Haven Moses for ten and I felt a little lift from the fans. A lot of
talking goes on right down on the field, and it helped when the
catcalls from the Seahawks bench were drowned out by a few
cheers. Two plays later and we were within striking distance. A
short pass to tackle Dave Studdard, who had come in at tight
end, quickly put us on the board. Score: 34–17.

As I ran off the field I yelled to linebacker Bob Swenson,
"Remember the Bears." Bob and I are alumni of the University
of California, and the Golden Bears had started out the 1979
season by making some spectacular comebacks against favored
opponents. Bob told me later that as he ran past me he
thought, "Give us one break and we'll be back in this." On
Seattle's first play Randy Gradishar blitzed and forced Zorn's
throw. Swenson picked it off. I was back in again with the type
of good field position that Weese had never had in the first
half. Weese had earned the role of "starting" quarterback by
working hard through the summer, while I, thirty-six years old,
had started slowly and hadn't begun to click. A teammate in

the best sense of the word, Norris had stopped in one day in midsummer to visit my business manager, Minetta Miller, and said to her, "I had a notion to call Craig and ask him if he wanted to work out with me." He was concerned about getting ready for camp. That's how Norris had won the starting job.

But, now, with two passes, we were on the eleven; Haven Moses promptly burned his man and gathered in a soft strike in the end zone. Scoreboard: 34–24. I thought to myself, "Well, you never know," and again yelled to Swenson, "Remember the Bears!"

An electric tension now gripped the stadium, from the turf all the way up to the top row of seats. At our lowest ebb, coaches Joe Collier and Red Miller had been pacing the sidelines, yelling "Hey, stay together," and now they were starting to jump. The orange defense knew Seattle could not stop our offensive, now that it was moving, so they began to believe it was foreordained that they in turn would stop the Seahawks. That and the intense pressure of the crowd smothered Zorn on his next series, and Seattle had to give up the ball again. A short punt put us on their thirty-five. So far it had taken a five-pass series and a three-pass series for both touchdowns. This time I decided to go for the quick strike: one pass to Upchurch and a score. After the conversion it was 34–31.

On the field, we hadn't forgotten Bob Peck, yet we weren't trying to "win it" for him, either. We were just playing football. But 75,000 hoarse voices were music to his ears. The next time we got the ball, at the beginning of the fourth quarter, we found ourselves edging toward the go-ahead touchdown. We had been down so long, and had come back so quickly, that the whole game, even the score, was a blur. Everyone sensed it: there was no stopping us. True to his philosophy, of going with the "hot hand," Coach Miller left me in charge. We drove to the Seattle one. I handed off to Rob Lytle off tackle, and against a deafening roar the young halfback dug his chin into the end zone. We were finally ahead and the crowd was in delirium, so much so that few noticed as Rob clambered to his feet and raced, with the ball clutched under his arm, to the south tunnel.

As Rob tells it, "It was the biggest thing I've ever done. Bob Peck was a great friend to me—he kept my spirits up when I was injured, and that was about every year since I came out of college. I used to think there was nothing I could ever do to repay him. Then, when I hit the ground in the end zone, I don't know, the good Lord just hit me and told me to jump up. I knew where Bob was, so I just ran over there and gave him the ball and told him I loved him."

When Bob died on October 11, 1979, just a few weeks later, I wondered if there was any meaning in his final painful days, his sudden passing from our lives. Could I believe that his life had a purpose for me, or that his death fit into some larger plan for his family? Or even that a football game might figure in that plan?

Oh, yes, we managed to win that game and the stories filled the papers for a couple of days. But then, as I've always said, even a dramatic game like this is soon forgotten. We had a glorious comeback, and it quickly passed. Bob Peck will not be forgotten.

There is something close to the core of our human nature that loves a comeback. And there are many words for it. It's David overcoming Goliath. It's Harry Truman defying the pollsters. It's a conversion, a complete turnaround, success when failure seems inevitable. And I think one of the basic attractions of sports is our wish to see in some small sample this power of the human spirit to face and triumph over impossible odds.

The underdog, the outcast, and the overlooked are our heroes. Rightly so, for even in the sports world we can admire—but not really love—the consistent and overwhelming winner. This is why heavily favored teams seldom enjoy being watched by a national TV audience; they know they are perfect setups for an upset, and they know that the true fan is most pleased when the upset occurs.

So I might confess at the start that I've always felt more comfortable as a player who is fighting back for his place in the sports world, rather than, occasionally, as a player who "has it made." As a matter of fact, I've always felt that as an athlete I've been just a little shy, in one way or another, of attaining my goals. Something has always eluded me. Physically I've had almost every conceivable injury a quarterback doesn't want to have, but through concentration and determination I've been able to overcome some tough circumstances.

This is why my vision of human beings comes down to their ability to *believe*. The philosophers talk about free will, or intelligence, or moral courage as the mark of human nature; I see it as the ability to keep coming back when down and out, when rejected, when up against impossible odds—when there is nothing left but the power of belief.

But I should tell you something about myself before you get the notion that these thoughts are either very deep or very novel. They come, in fact, from rubbing elbows with some very fine people and from going through some difficult tests in life. I think that you and I are enough alike that you can put yourself in my shoes and see why I have come to believe what I have.

Before I was of school age my family had made several moves—from Flint, Michigan, where I was born on February 5, 1943, to the Central Valley in California, finally settling in Campbell, a quiet suburb on the San Francisco peninsula. My father was a glass blower by trade; like many another young family in those postwar days, we traveled wherever his opportunities took him. As it turned out, his last move during my childhood was very fortuitous for me: first, in terms of the opportunities for development in sports that were waiting for me at Campbell, and second, in terms of the dedicated Campbell teachers whose impact on me may have remained subliminal for many years but finally made its mark.

This simple fact of my own upbringing seems as clear to me now as a pass pattern, but I don't think we have yet learned how critical it is. What we teach youngsters, by example or personal instruction, will always be with them. It may take years to surface, for good or ill. We have no way of measuring its effects. Yet that early impression means everything to the future of our world.

If this sounds like another platitude, think of it this way: We discourage rather than encourage dedication among

elementary school teachers. We battle about the high cost of
school programs. We accept the deterioration of child-parent-
teacher involvement as a part of modern society. I'm not
proposing any solutions here. I'm simply asking you to recall
your own upbringing, as I'm doing now, and think about what
you might have become without the childhood influences you
inherited.

For someone like me, who has remained in sports for all
his adult life, the importance of teachers is magnified. Even
the most jaded professional athlete knows the difference
between a strong coach and a phony. (Children, by the way,
know the same thing about their teachers.) Athletes aren't any
more "childish" than their counterparts in other lines of adult
business or work, just because they "play" a "game." All of us,
I believe, continue to grow as human beings, or we die in spirit,
if not in fact. In any case, I've come into contact with teachers
all my life, whether you call them that or call them coaches,
trainers, or ministers. Three coaches who have influenced my
life are the subjects of later chapters in this book. One of the
things I have learned from them all is simply that there is no
book, no vision, no experience that means as much to a
person's growth as a teacher.

Occasionally I tell my friends about my grammar school
coach, Bruce Stevenson, and they say, "You mean sports are
so big in California that you have coaches in grammar school?"
Then I have to explain that Bruce is really "only" a teacher.
But he took his teaching so seriously that he was also a
counselor, coach, surrogate parent—and friend—to every
fourth grader he met. He got hooked on total involvement
when he was young, so now he couldn't change if he wanted to!

In high school I was coached by Jim Muir in football,
John Oldham in baseball, and Burt Robinson in basketball.
Between them they're responsible for whatever talent I had
when I was ready for college. They probably knew more about
my future than I did—I thought I could be a baseball star!
Major league scouts looked me over and suggested several
interesting possibilities—all involving skipping college. My
dad and I gave it a lot of thought. I was eager to leave the
confines of a strict household, which I shared with two sisters,

Sharon and Sandy, and see the world for myself as rapidly as possible. Yet as much as I was anxious to play left field for a farm club in Yakima or Duluth, I wanted much more to go on to college, so I accepted a football scholarship to the University of California at Berkeley—or, as it is more succinctly known in the West, at "Cal."

My father was a disciplinarian when it came to raising kids; I'll have a lot to say about how I rebelled against authority for at least a dozen years after leaving my home. But I guess he got through to me in other ways, too. He knew that the San Francisco Forty-Niners were "my" team. I couldn't wait for football season to roll around, so I could watch Y. A. Tittle throw to Billy Wilson and Hugh McElhenny break away from tacklers in an open field. The duels between Bob Waterfield of the Rams and Tittle were a sort of world championship in my book. Then one day my dad, who was in charge of entertainment for a kids' sports banquet, arranged for Billy Wilson to be the guest speaker, and I met one of my idols face to face. Perhaps my father knew that this sort of thing would eventually steer me toward football. And in most cases, to make a career in football one had to go to college.

All this time I was surrounded by religion, in one form or another, but it made no conscious impression on me. I saw "the Lord," as I would say now, but of course couldn't then, in a man like Bruce Stevenson. Like most men, I felt my mother had the strongest emotional role in my life, and she influenced me spiritually. The major social events of our community were centered at the Methodist Church. But the Bible remained for me just another relic of a bygone era, full of old fairy tales and harsh moralizing. From now on, anything that smacked of authority was something to smack back.

Physically I was on top of the world. I came to the right college team at the right time, and I could do no wrong—on the field. Now, more than fifteen years later, only one of my "all-time" records remains unbroken at Cal, but I held quite a few for many years. I didn't do badly on the baseball diamond, either; my health was excellent, I had a good pair of eyes, and I had inherited a strong throwing arm from one of the Mortons. How meaningless the statistics are now; then, stats were an all-important ticket to the big show: pro football. I was drafted number one by the Dallas Cowboys—and also by the Oakland Raiders.

In those days the Raiders were struggling along in the AFL and played at a sort of unsheltered park with portable stands called Frank Youell Field. In contrast, the Cowboys were playing in the Cotton Bowl stadium, were about to be contenders in the long-established NFL, and had a recruitment program that was classier than that of a Big Ten college. (Yes, the colleges had to teach the pros how to recruit an athlete.) All the social advantages of living in Dallas and being part of the Cowboy organization were drummed into a young man's head with frequent visits and letters. Before long, if they really wanted you, you had collected so many items of clothing and trinkets with the Dallas insignia on them that you began to believe you were already a Cowboy. To top it all off, Dallas was a faraway place and Oakland was my backyard; there was no question where I would go.

Now a strange malaise came over me. In high school and college I could do no wrong; with luck and the right physical equipment I achieved the best there was to have. But when I became a pro I began to feel like "Mr. Almost." There was no great shock of discovery; I wasn't suddenly disillusioned the way you might think Pete Gent or Dave Meggysey were. Both men were good players and good writers, and they fit in well with the anti-everything mood of the country in the late sixties. Their books showed their frustration with a game that had given them a fairly good living and an opportunity to make an even better one with the publicity that comes with the turf. Perhaps they resented the fact that team owners were doing far better than the players, and they didn't have to chase up and down the field and break their noses like gladiators. No, I felt I was in the football business by choice; besides, I enjoyed the game! My problem was that I wasn't ready to commit myself emotionally and mentally to the leaders in professional sports the way I had thrown myself into amateur athletics.

I got a glimmering of the professional attitude when I was being recruited by the Raiders. Al Davis told me he didn't want to offer me a contract because he had heard I had already signed with Dallas. I told him I hadn't. But the Raiders remained skeptical, and there was nothing I could do to convince them I was being straight with them. An innocent athlete also gets a shock of realization when it sinks in that this is entertainment, not just a game. An old friend of mine once told me about his first year in the minor leagues as a pitcher. During the exhibition season he turned in five hitless innings one day, and happened to meet the big brass, the owners of the entire organization, as he left the locker room. Expecting some sort of compliment, he introduced himself; they must know him by face, he thought, because they had been sitting behind first base all afternoon. They shook hands, then one of them said to the other, "What was the gate today?"

The professional game is also rougher than college football, but that's much easier to adjust to. Above all, football is mental. Any athlete can suffer pain and possible injury if his heart is in it. A long-distance runner has to be prepared to push himself beyond his limits: immediately after a killing marathon, a runner may vow never to run again. A quarterback can expect the pent-up wrath of opposing linemen, not to mention the jeers and insults of his own fans when things go wrong. When the great halfback Walter Payton and the Chicago Bears had a rough day against San Diego, 40–7, in 1979, he told reporters, "You got a son? Well, keep him away from football. It's too much abuse to your body. It'll mess up your life." By the end of the season Walter was leading the Bears to a thrilling, last-minute division title.

Well, my mental attitude was a long time in adjusting to the demands of pro football. I always held something back, never trusting myself to make a full commitment. It was a sort of skepticism about the values of the game, my coaches, and my fellow players. In a small way, I was unwilling to believe in what I was doing.

The first few years of pro football for most new quarterbacks are spent understudying the veteran. In my case I had to watch Don Meredith from the bench and engage in friendly competition with Jerry Rhome for a chance at the starting assignment. Meredith in turn had won his job from Eddie LeBaron, the little magician. Finally, in my fourth year with the Cowboys, Dandy Don decided it was time to turn his many talents to better use in the media, and I got my chance. Unfortunately, I also got my first major injury in pro football; in a game in Atlanta in 1969 I suffered a shoulder separation when I was sacked from the blind side. And a tendon had to be transplanted from my left foot to my right shoulder in my throwing arm, and a subsequent elbow operation was necessary because of the shoulder injury. Turning point number one.

A young man named Roger Staubach came into my life in a big way. Actually he was my senior by one year to the day, having done a hitch in the Navy while under a long-term Cowboy contract. He was a twenty-seven-year-old rookie in 1969, when he took over for me in a few games after I jammed a finger of my right hand on a tackler's helmet. This was the beginning of a long, friendly-enemies competition for the top spot at Dallas. When I continued to have problems with my arm as the 1970 season opened, Roger began to challenge me just when I thought I had overcome the resistance of the veteran, Meredith, and won a clear right to the quarterback job. When I look back now on pictures of Roger, Don, and me at training camp, I can read the future in our looks: Meredith, who might well have been classed with the best in pro football history if he had a few breaks, is bored; Staubach is out to prove something; and I'm groping for something.

A curious feature of our competition at this time was that Coach Landry and Roger shared a certain religious viewpoint, as we will see. They crossed denominational lines in a firm conviction that their Christian belief was worth bringing to other people. Meanwhile, I was considered something of a playboy. True, I was a bachelor. True, I was basking in the adulation of a sports-conscious city, and I was enjoying it. I had also received some notoriety from a situation that should have made me look like a country hick. I was forced to declare bankruptcy about that time because of my blind faith in some business partners in California. When I was in college I had always wanted to be involved with books in one way or another—even as a writer. I got my chance when some real money came my way in signing with Dallas; I went in with a

classmate in buying U.C. Corner, one of the landmark bookstores close by the U.C. campus. Soon we had expanded to a
bookstore/coffeeshop operation at the University of California
at Davis. Trusting the business judgment of my partners
explicitly, I pledged six years of my salary to the business. I
would play football and leave the day-to-day operation of the
bookstores to my buddies. Unfortunately, good business sense
wasn't their strong point either, and things began to sour.
Before I knew what was happening, bill collectors were coming
to me for payment. I went to the business office of the
Cowboys for advice, and they told me to bail out. I had been
victimized by being too trusting, but when people read "bankruptcy" and "business ventures" in the newspapers they conjured up a vision of a high-flying, free-wheeling spender who
dabbled in quarterbacking on the side.

To their everlasting credit, there was not a chance that
either Landry or Staubach, being the type of men they were,
would use anything but good football judgment in playing and
coaching the game. But it set people thinking. Ludicrous
though it may seem, people began to take sides about the
"Bible Belt" within the Dallas organization. Anything for
controversy—anything for scandal. Recently, a highly publicized film, *North Dallas Forty,* played on the same theme. In
fact, wild parties and self-righteous prayer meetings were both
very scarce in our lives. Football was our living.

The pressure of competing for the starting quarterback
job grew as intense as the pressure on Landry to win. In
admiring Landry by including him in this book I don't mean to
imply that I ever got along with his way of driving his teams.
While I don't think he consciously tried to intimidate us, I do
know what the effect was. The Monday morning post-mortems
of the previous day's game were so pressure-packed that even
the veterans cringed when the films began to roll. I confess
that my insides churned so much that I had to spend many a
session in the bathroom—and the fear scarcely abated throughout my nine and a half years with the team. It's difficult to
explain how a young man can desire so desperately to play the
game, and yet know how humiliated and defeated he will be
made to feel when things go wrong. Why not sit on the bench

and collect your salary? They don't show film clips of the bench.

Well, believe it: Roger and I both wanted to play, desperately. When I was rolling through a fairly successful 1969–70 season, he asked to be traded to a team like Atlanta. I had gone through the same feeling, and was on the verge of packing up and leaving, when Meredith took "early retirement." Because of injuries, both of us had a chance to show our wares. Then, in the 1971 season, both of us were relatively healthy and the competition between us came to a head. I would play one game, he'd start the next. There were even a few disasters on our home field, and the fans would scream for the return of Dandy Don! The indecision reached ridiculous heights when Landry announced before the Chicago game that he would alternate quarterbacks on every play!

Here was another turning point in my career as a person as well as a football player. The game seesawed, just like the quarterbacks, with Chicago holding a one-touchdown edge late in the fourth quarter. Landry had decided to send in all the plays during the 1970 season, "to take the responsibility off the quarterback," and now he was sending in quarterbacks *with* the plays. His reasoning was that he could thereby give the quarterback a full briefing on his thinking. All of a sudden, he reversed himself and left me in to try to rescue the game. I had the plays and a great team to work with, but again I fell short. The Bears held us off, 23–19. In my heart I knew something was missing from my play, from my commitment to the game. The sportswriters assumed that I was the starting quarterback because Landry had stayed with me in the clutch, but I knew different. During the following week he announced that he was now going with Staubach.

Roger took full advantage of his opportunity. Starting with a 4–3 record, he led the Cowboys to the NFC championship and a crack at the Super Bowl—number six. To everyone's surprise we overwhelmed a strong Miami team, as I looked on from the bench. Super Bowl VI in New Orleans immediately vaulted Staubach into the rarefied atmosphere of a superstar, and, as much as I liked him and his style of play, I wanted to be more than a reserve to a superstar. What did I want? The clippings, the torrent of superlatives from sports-writers, the hero worship of millions of kids? Perhaps. But mainly I wanted to prove myself.

I suffered through a long winter and a training camp that gave every sign of my continued decline into the role of backup. My arm had fully healed by now. I began to think in terms of being traded. Then the fates showed why champion-ship teams require backup in every position. In an exhibition game with the Los Angeles Rams, Roger was carried away with the spirit of the game and tried to scramble out of a broken play to a first down. He got the first down, all right, but also a painful shoulder separation in his left shoulder. A difficult operation was finally decided upon and was successful—but, like my injury the year before, this one would haunt Roger for the rest of the season. Almost.

With only an occasional assist from Staubach, I was able to quarterback the Cowboys to another spot in the playoffs—not as a division or conference champion, but as a wild card with a 10–4 record. We had to play the San Francisco Forty-Niners two days before Christmas for the *right* to play for the NFC championship. This was a team we had beaten in the regular season at Dallas, but the handwriting was on the wall when Vic Washington took the opening kickoff ninety-seven yards for a touchdown. We tried to play catch-up for the rest of the afternoon. When the Forty-Niners recovered a fumble on our one-yard line in the third quarter, and quickly pushed the ball in, the score stood at 28–13. The fans at Candlestick Park sensed a victory, and the catcalls from the opposite bench became more raucous. We managed to put a field goal on the board to make it 28–16. Then a strange thing happened.

Man for man, play for play, we could tell the 'Niners wanted to go home and enjoy a holiday dinner. They became conservative. We could count on three plays and a punt. They didn't have to score to win, did they? Finally we got the ball back with a little less than two minutes to play and I felt that old comeback feeling in my bones. Only, Landry sent Stau-bach in!

San Francisco, the team I idolized in my youth, would not be my opponent in this last moment of drama. I couldn't even watch Roger's first pass, but it was complete. We took a time out, then threw two more passes complete with a quick lineup between them. Suddenly we were at the San Francisco twenty. I looked at the clock: one minute and fifteen seconds left. During the time out, Landry said, "The post to Parks will be open." Roger hit Billy Parks after a tremendous move to make it 28–23 with the conversion.

The fans who had begun to leave the park now jammed the exits, standing impatiently for the final score to be posted. The only "possibility" was a successful on-side kick. But the possible happened. Mel Renfro pounced on the ball when it squirted free of the grasp of the Forty-Niner front wall on the kickoff. Staubach promptly darted up the middle for twenty yards on the first play from scrimmage: the whole defense had spread open, looking for a deep pass. Next Roger called a corner route and completed at the ten, his receiver stepping out of bounds to stop the clock. Time was no longer going against us. Staubach decided to go to the sidelines again, but a blitz was on and he quickly fired it over the middle for a touchdown. I ran out onto the field and lifted Roger into the air in the biggest bear hug I've given anyone. And we still had thirty seconds on the clock! But this was *our* comeback, and the final score read Dallas 30, San Francisco 28.

Landry couldn't contain himself. "This is the greatest comeback we've ever had," he yelled to reporters. Three days later, back on our practice field, he announced that Staubach was now the Cowboys quarterback for the playoffs. Comeback? Not for me.

It turned out that there would not be a Super Bowl VII for us, for we were soundly beaten by the Washington Redskins the following week, 26–3. Roger played the game out to its bitter conclusion. For me it was turning point number two: I had lost my starting job in one minute and a half of a playoff game, and even a mediocre performance by my successor changed nothing. The whole 1972 season became fixed in my mind as an exercise in futility.

In training camp and during the exhibition season in 1973, Roger and I were at each other's throats again—figuratively. Both of us knew it was somewhat of a battle of statistics,

Landry being the pragmatist he is. I ended the preseason with a strong game against Miami, and felt I had earned the starting assignment. I suspect that Roger was equally confident, yet he threatened to ask to be traded if he had to play second fiddle for the Cowboys. It was also contract time for many of us, and I had my troubles in coming to terms. But the real payoff was on the field. Landry bided his time, as he always does, then announced his decision quietly. He was going with Roger. He kept telling me, "I've got this feeling," when I asked him why he had more confidence in Staubach.

I had a feeling, too. I begged to be traded, and Landry begged me to wait. I threw maybe thirty passes in all our games, and my contribution to our winning season was nothing in my mind. When the season ended short of the Super Bowl, I couldn't feel pride or sorrow. Someone read me a stirring call by Theodore Roosevelt:

> *Far better it is to dare mighty things, to win glorious triumphs, even though checkered by failure, than to take rank with those poor spirits who neither enjoy much nor suffer much, because they live in that gray twilight that knows not victory nor defeat.*

I didn't know an awful lot about Teddy, but I did know that the "gray twilight" was not for me. I kept pressing Landry to resolve the eternal dilemma: play me or trade me. When the 1974 season started and I was still clutching the bench in a so-so performance by Roger, I took the matter to Tex Schramm, the president of the Cowboys. Within two days of not showing up for Monday morning practice, I was traded to the New York Giants. I left many good friends behind in Dallas, but at last I was on my way to freedom—I thought.

The Giants were as disorganized as the Cowboys were regimented. Coach Bill Arnsbarger was a great guy, but he had inherited a chaotic system. In an every-man-for-himself situation, I tried to go out and prove that a quarterback could do it on his own. How wrong I was. I tried to force plays, and found myself throwing off balance, running against the tide. I was "daring mighty events," all right, but the "checkering with failure" was becoming a whitewash. I staggered through the rest of the 1974 season, hoping for a turnaround the following year. It didn't come then, or the year after. The "fans" would line up outside the steel fence separating the crowd from the path to the dressing room, and dress us down with hearty expletives as we skulked by. The cussing out I got every Sunday started to get vicious. New York City wasn't Dallas! What kind of a living was this, I thought, if it depended on the approval of nothing less than a mob of hateful people?

The few bright spots in this dismal episode were reunions with old teammates after games and the occasional visits of someone who had confidence in me,—a young lady from Dallas named Suzie. Since my first few successful seasons as a starter at Dallas, everything had gone downhill. Yet I had learned something about myself: I wasn't afraid. I didn't take any credit for this sort of moral courage; it seemed to come naturally. No matter how much I was battered, I went back up to the line of scrimmage as if the game had just been invented. And at New York, many of us felt it *had.*

In a small way, football teaches us that everything we do is noticed by someone, even if that someone is only an opposing player or coach. The same thing is true in a much bigger way in life itself—yet we seldom act on that knowledge. We perform only for the immediate boss, or to accomplish the immediate assignment. It sometimes takes a game like football to impress this lesson on people. For twelve long years I had waited for "somone up there" to notice me and help me find my niche. Suddenly, along came that person. A coach of the New England Patriots, Red Miller, took over at Denver. He remembered my playing on the frozen fields of the East; he needed a seasoned quarterback to bring that elusive quality, leadership, to a young Bronco squad. When he approached me, it was like catching the last train out of Siberia. In 1977 I would play for a team that wanted me—no, *needed* me.

For every type of personality there is a coach to bring out the best, and for me that coach was Miller. When I reported to Denver I felt that I had been released from a steaming jungle into a tropical lagoon. Everything was relaxed, yet the men showed up for the first workout "clean shaven and in good shape," as Red expressed it. They meant business, I saw at once. I want to be part of this good feeling, I told Suzie, who came up from Dallas looking better than ever. Now we had a chance to talk, instead of simply go out on the town. I began to feel that I was more than just another date for her—and something else, too. She talked to me about her new commitment to "the Lord."

As much as I had shared private conversations with Tom Landry and Roger Staubach, two of the most outspoken Christians I had every met, the closest I had come to Christ and the Lord and God was when fans swore at me. Believe me, the foulest-mouthed linebackers in the league can't match a drunken "fan" for vile language. I admired the strong faith of my Cowboy coach and major rival, but admiration isn't action. I thought a lot about the dedicated service of Bruce Stevenson to grammar school kids. But until Suzie shared her feelings with me about the things that matter most in life, I looked on religion as just another cloak of authority. I wanted to be free! I wanted to conquer the world on my own two feet! I didn't need a crutch.

As the training camp and preseason showed me more about my new coach and a whole range of different players I had never known before, a change came over me. Guys like Randy Gradishar, Barney Chavez, Rubin Carter, and Steve Foley had a more serious bent than I had seen in other football players. Jack Dolbin told me about his awakening to the message of the Bible. Coach Miller kept his religious commitment to himself, but it shone through anyway. Instead of an atmosphere of fear, there was a climate of confidence, as if we were no longer college kids playing a game but adults preparing for a battle. It was like pilgrims arriving in the New World; we were being given a new lease on life. Or, I should say, *I* was being given a new lease on life, in my head as well as on the field.

The phrase "born again" had been around for some time, but I was hazy about exactly what it meant. I guess it was associated mostly with the title of a book by one of the Watergate scandal people, Charles Colson. He had found Christianity as a result of being shaken from power and made to face his life all over again—from prison. Many of my

teammates said they were born-again Christians, so I thought
they meant they had reformed or had some mystical insight
into religion. They didn't walk around with halos over their
heads or "turn the other cheek" on the football field, but I
suspected all sorts of crazy things. They probably believed in
faith healing, speaking in tongues, or laying on of hands, I
thought.

Then Suzie laid it out to me plain and simple: To be born
again simply means to have a spiritual life as well as a physical
life. She explained the story in the New Testament about
Nicodemus—John 3: this Jewish ruler told Jesus that he could
see that God was with him because of all the signs he was
giving. Christ answered, "Yes, unless you are born again, you
won't see God's kingdom." This answer put Nicodemus, obviously a literal man, in a quandary. He answered, "How can a
man be born again when he's old? Can he go back to the womb
and be reborn?" To paraphrase Christ's patient answer:
"Don't let it bother you when I say you've got to be born
again—whatever is born of a body is a body, and whatever is
born of the Spirit is spirit." The dialog continued, with Nicodemus still playing dumb. Christ said, in effect, "You're supposed to be a teacher and you can't understand the difference
between the physical and the spiritual?" So the message about
being reborn is quite simple: You're "reborn" when your
spiritual life begins, whether that happens at the time of your
baptism or, in my case, when you suddenly wake up to the
spiritual side of life, accepting Jesus Christ as your personal
Savior.

So I didn't have any startling conversion—I wasn't knocked
off my horse, like St. Paul, by a bolt from the blue. I just began
to see the effect of a spiritual life on friends around me,
football players and coaches who I *knew* weren't crazy! And
Suzie's enthusiasm for her newfound faith meant even more to
me, because I had known her as a nonbeliever. I went with her
to Bible discussions, even though the mere mention of the
Bible had always turned me off. I discovered that the Bible,
both the New and the Old Testament, was far from the
mysterious, cultish relic I had always imagined it to be. I got
over my cynical attitude toward words like "spirit" and "the

Word." A football player would have to be blind indeed not to know the value of spirit—or what the coach meant when he said what the word from management was!

I had done a lot of reading—which was one of the reasons I originally got involved in the bookstore business: what you like you think *everyone* must like. Yet I had never read the Bible as a real, honest-to-goodness book. I began to see Christ as a real person. What struck me most was his compassion, his ability to comfort and heal, mentally as well as physically. In that same story of Nicodemus, Jesus goes on to say, "For God did not send his son into the world to condemn the world, but to save it."

Lord knows, I needed comforting after being knocked around the NFC. Now, reading the Bible with Suzie and other friends, I began to see that comfort isn't a winning season, a Super Bowl, a penthouse in Manhattan's Upper East Side. As much as I had shunned the "good word" because it was called hokey things like that, now I saw it really *was* the good word. It made sense.

Against this backdrop, even football began to fall into place for me. Now, get me right: the last thing that I thought the Bible would do for me was help me play football. I know that fads often sweep professional sports, just as they go through the general population: transcendental meditation, the relaxation response, yoga. People consciously use these devices to improve their business or professional abilities. Some people try to use religion as a sort of TM or mind-expanding or tension-relaxing technique. When the San Francisco Giants baseball team of a few years back had four or five starters talking to reporters every day about "the Lord," some columnists suggested that this too was part of the fad. Prayer meetings were held before every game, both in football and baseball, by some teams. It's probably true that the inner peace that such activities promoted was good for many players: it helped them forget their troubles and concentrate on the thing at hand. If that's all that it was, it was indeed just a fad. I believe in giving everyone the benefit of the doubt, and I assume that most athletes don't try to "use" religion to improve their game. In my case, I know that whether I played another

game of football or not in 1977, I had found in Christ a purpose
and a direction for my life, and, most important, eternal life.

How different I was many years before, playing for Dallas
against Baltimore in Super Bowl V. With the score 13–13,
I tried to win it in the last minutes, but my pass glanced off
Dan Reeves' hands into the arms of the Colts' middle line-
backer, Mike Curtis, for an interception. As time ran out,
Baltimore moved into field goal range. That time I prayed to
God that the Colts wouldn't make it. (They did.) That was my
idea of prayer then.

Bill Russell said something on this subject in his own
inimitable way, in his recent memoirs, *Second Wind*. He was in
a jam, and, though he professes not to be deeply religious, he
thought of asking God for help:

> *Usually on such occasions I have one of my infrequent
> conversations with God. I tell Him and if He'll just get
> me out of this one scrape, He'll never have to worry
> about me again.*

I felt that my God-given arm would take care of me on the
football field. But I also discovered that, with my life in better
order and with my values in better perspective, I couldn't help
but do my work more effectively. Red Miller's approach to the
game coincided beautifully with my new self-awareness. He
concentrated on playing to our strengths. As an excellent
offensive strategist, he talked my language. Above all, he was
fair. Whatever he coaches, he will be all these things.

As the 1977 season unfolded, it became clear that we had
another strength that would become the mark of the team: the
Orange Crush defense. Our linebackers, like Bob Swenson,
Tom Jackson, Joe Rizzo, and Randy Gradishar, had the mo-
bility to patrol a wide area, so we could drop one more man off
the line to double-team receivers. And we could afford to blitz
more. The Orange Crush became synonymous with forcing
turnovers, on sacks and interceptions. It makes quite a difference to the offense when it comes in at midfield instead of
around its own twenty. Sportscasters are fond of talking about
field position, but that's just an abstract phrase that any
school kid knows better as "closer to the goal." Look at it this

way: if the offense makes a mistake in one play out of ten, by failing to make a third-down conversion, or committing a turnover from a fumble or interception, then the chances of scoring from the fifty are double or triple the chances of scoring from your own twenty. When teams are leg-tired in the second half, those thirty yards are sometimes like Normandy Beach on D-Day.

We knew we were on the road to a conference title when we overcame Pittsburgh in mid-November. That Sunday was slightly more memorable for me, however, for a different reason. Right after the game I went to Dallas, and before about a thousand friends Suzie and I went to the altar. I think those who knew me well realized that this was something special, because they came from New York, from California, and all points between to help celebrate our wedding day. I had never suspected that there were that many true friends out there; I have never before been so honored, and don't expect to be again. I had come late to understanding myself, late to knowing the Lord, and late to family life. As we'll see in the case of Roger Staubach, all three usually coincide, early or late.

The crucial game that year was the last one with our perennial rival and conference champions, the Oakland Raiders. But this time we had them in Mile High Stadium, this time we had the Orange Crush, and this time the steady hand of Red Miller was guiding our fortunes. On a controversial play, Rob Lytle recovered a fumble that would have stopped our drive inside the Raider five; we went on to score and close out the game with a ferocious defensive effort. When the playoff dust settled, we found ourselves in our first Super Bowl—against my old teammates, the Cowboys. No one expected us to withstand Staubach and a precision-drilled Landry organization. As often happens to first-time Super Bowl contestants, the thrill of being there sapped our competitive strength. In losing a lackluster game, however, we didn't lose our pride. Victory would have been sweet after the nine-and-a-half-year "sibling rivalry" between Roger and me, but it wouldn't have proved anything. I surprised a lot of reporters and former teammates afterwards by saying I accepted the loss as part of the Lord's plan. We were not to be champions of the world that

year, but at the same time that was the professional highlight
of my life.

Some years before, when I was with Dallas, I had been
invited to write a guest article for the *Dallas Morning News*,
and there I had the opportunity to explain what football
meant, and didn't mean, to my life, and what my personal
beliefs meant, and didn't mean, to football. But now I knew far
more.

The following year was the end of the honeymoon in
Denver. Wisely, Miller emphasized the team rather than the
individual, so when I started slowly and failed to move the
offense consistently, he called on Norris Weese. The fan is a
fickle creature: I went from hero to goat in a few short months.
A cycle began to appear. As several sportswriters pointed out,
I could be king one moment and a candidate for being run out
of town on a rail the next moment. But in my heart I knew I had
beaten the fear-of-success syndrome that in earlier years had
denied me full victory. I was giving everything I could; "almost"
had gone out of my lexicon. Then what was the matter? There
are simply too many variables in a quarterback's performance
for anyone to say when or why he will have a bad day. A
dropped pass here, a missed block there, and the whole course
of a game can change. The fans don't want to hear about what
might have been—they want results. So someone has to be
pinpointed for blame. Certain characteristics in a player, however, can be detected by an experienced observer. Recently I
was cheered to read the following analysis by that great quarterback who preceded me at Cal, Joe Kapp:

> *That's the factor that people tend to ignore—the
> supporting cast. Bart Starr of the Packers was good
> but look at the guys around him. Same with Ken
> Stabler, although I have the greatest respect for Sta-
> bler's poise in pressure situations. The guy who's
> always been underrated is Craig Morton. He plays hurt
> and throws a beautiful ball.*

I remember following Kapp's exploits for the Golden Bears
when he led them to the 1959 Rose Bowl—which was then the
Super Bowl in every young man's mind. I was still in high school

at the time. I never dreamed that some twenty years later he would throw me such a nice bone. "Plays hurt and throws a beautiful ball." I'll take it.

For several games in that wobbly 1978 season, Coach Miller had to resort to alternating quarterbacks. When Weese cooled off, I was tapped on the shoulder. In a memorable game against Pittsburgh, I fell behind early and the score seemed unsurmountable. Norris then came on like a tiger, and I had visions of another Staubach comeback, right down to the last-minute on-side kickoff. Only this time, on the final play of the game, we couldn't nudge it in from the one. But we caught fire as the season went along, and I regained the starting role. Over one stretch toward the end of the season I threw 144 passes without an interception, and quite a string of completions in a row. Again we bounced Oakland out of conference contention, but in the playoffs our Super Bowl hopes were quickly snuffed out.

In many ways a similar pattern occurred in 1979, except that this time Weese established himself early as our starter and I was called on only in desperation. Desperation it was in the Seattle game mentioned at the beginning of this chapter—the "impossible" comeback so heartbreakingly intertwined with the last days of Bob Peck. That game gave me another opportunity to rescue myself from early retirement; Coach Miller stayed with me as long as I could move the ball, and we backed into the playoffs, not as division champs this time, but as a wild card. Among the ironies that are an inherent feature of this pressure-packed sport, on successive weekends Jim Zorn and the Seahawks nipped us and overpowered the Raiders—first leaving us dangling in search of a playoff berth, and then snatching playoff hopes from Oakland. This was the team we stunned in our great game early in the season, with my old buddy and rival, Jerry Rhome, coaching the offense.

If you know me a little better now, after following the course of my up-and-down professional life, perhaps you can appreciate a little better the impact that Christ has made on my way of thinking. In spite of an image I might have projected in the past as a playboy, or as a super-confident athlete, or as a controversial troublemaker, underneath that media-created man has always been a naive, unsure, ambitious, puzzled boy.

The calmness and poise that Christ brought into my life has, I'm happy to report, been picked up by observers of the sports scene. Joseph Sanchez of the *Denver Post* caught some of this in an interview midway through the 1978 season, just after I started to come out of the early-season doldrums. "I don't care to be controversial," I told him, "and I don't want to do or say anything that would be disruptive to the team. Besides, I really don't think anything I have to say is all that interesting." Well, we talked about football, because Joe is, after all, a sportswriter, but we also touched on life and love—things just as important to a sportswriter as to a jock. Then he wrote, with a bow to my old image:

> *A reformed rowdy, Morton has become a very private person since his conversion to Christianity a year and a half ago. He would rather have a quiet conversation with friends, but when he does agree to an interview, most of what he has to say—contrary to his opinion—is of more than passing interest.*

There's a double meaning in that last phrase that I hope is revealing. If I have become an "enigma" to many fans, as Woodrow Paige, Jr. claimed in a story in the *Rocky Mountain News* that year, maybe it's because I'm now trying to be more than a football player. The tension between the game and my personal life is something like the movement of two geological masses along an earthquake fault. At some point there's going to be a quake. Part of the problem, of course, is the win-at-all-costs mentality of the average fan. Paige writes:

> *Morton gets out of a hospital bed to decimate Oakland in the conference championship game and could run for governor. He throws four interceptions as the Denver Broncos are destroyed in the Super Bowl, and the only thing he could run for was his life.*

Then he quotes, but not by name, two people who he says know me well:

> *. . . Craig doesn't want attention, but he can't prevent it, by the things he does in and out of football.*
> *. . . He's either one of them (Christians) or one of us (the others), but he can't be both.*

These are honest opinions, to which I can only answer: The only attention I want is that which will help me share the joy I've found in a belief in Christ; and that belief is not inconsistent with being quite a normal human being, warts and all. In today's world it takes courage to speak out for what you believe in, for the media can bring your detractors to your doorstep pretty fast. Anyone in professional sports, whether he likes it or not, is a model to the public. Sometimes he's a model of tenacity, teamwork, or leadership. Sometimes he's a model of poor sportsmanship or pettiness. In the male-dominated field of professional sports, the athlete often stands as a demonstration of the idea that being rough and tough is what it takes to be a man. Only he-men are men. This would only be Monday-morning quarterbacking except for the fact that *a whole generation* of Americans is being raised, influenced, formed by what they see on Sunday afternoons on television, rather than on Sunday mornings in church.

What youngsters see in pro football may be fierce competition and a degree of violence, but I don't think either is all that bad or distorted in the entire picture. What I object to is the unconscious statement made by the exclusion of positive qualities from the screen: the statement that religion and the qualities expressed in the life of Christ are not for real men and women, real athletes. If all a child ever learned about an athlete is that he hits hard, lives hard, and throws his helmet hard when he loses, that child is surely getting a one-sided view of his models.

Athletes often show heart—that element which is the difference between a winner and a loser when all else is fairly equal. Heart is a close relative of courage, as Bill Russell so carefully distinguishes in his memoirs:

> *For the champion it is a test of heart. Heart in champions is a funny thing. People mistake it for courage, though there's no moral element in it. To me, you display courage when you take a stand for something you believe to be morally right, and do so in the face of adversity or danger. That's not what sports is about. Heart in champions has to do with depth of motivation, and how well your mind and body react to pressure.*

So what I'm saying is I want more than "sports courage" to be seen on the tube; I want a little "life courage" to be there too. Not during a roll-out, nor a time-out, nor even in locker-room interviews. But athletes should give a broader view of their beliefs *throughout* the media—as citizens, as parents, as taxpayers, or as consumers. To paraphrase a famous analysis of war, the welfare of the nation is too important to be left to the politicians.

We can't run away from trials and struggles in life, because they are what build courage. I think Bill Russell would agree, on the same reasoning, that heart, or depth of motivation, also doesn't fall from the blue. Walt Whitman said it long ago, but it bears repeating all the time in our comfort-conscious world: "It takes struggles in life to make strength; it takes fight for principles to make fortitude; it takes crisis to give courage and singleness of purpose to reach any objective." High-sounding platitudes, you might say, if all you ever did was watch prime-time television. For the message of our media is that happiness comes from avoiding any possible crisis or controversy. I would like to see that point of view tempered by the experience of athletes—*outside* their uniforms. The power of television, especially, is widely underrated; I know of dozens of cases where the message of the Bible somehow got through to people from a chance flipping of the dial to a "Sunday morning" type program. Vince DiMaggio, who with Dom and Joe was part of the finest brother act in baseball, tells an illuminating story about his own born-again experience. His wife, Madeline, turned to a Billy Graham program one evening. Vince complained, "Isn't there anything else on but that?" But Madeline wanted to listen for a while. Vince read the newspaper when the same program continued the next night, and the next. But something must have found its way into his ears, because, as he relates it:

> *Suddenly, I was out of my chair and down on my knees.*
> *I don't really know how I got there. I wasn't myself. But*
> *there I was on my knees, crying, and right there in our*
> *den I accepted the Lord.*

I'm sure this kind of confession brings a silly smile to most faces, if not an out-and-out snicker. Baseball heroes don't cry, first of all; they don't fall on their knees except to make a diving catch; and they don't believe something moves them other than themselves. "Accepting the Lord" also sounds so pious, as if it were a secret initiation ceremony or a mystical pact. We don't go around talking about accepting the President or accepting the United Nations. If I said I accepted my wife you might think I considered her a great burden. So the words put us off, once again. Christians may come to know the meaning of this sort of acceptance, but it creates artificial hurdles among people who never use the word that way.

Another great barrier that should be swept aside is the confusing array of religious denominations and their occasional squabbles. Even in this ecumenical age, when we're supposed to be open to the practices of other religions, the mere *existence* of so many sects and churches gives *all* religious beliefs a curious coloring. I don't want to get into a discussion of what is the "true" Church or who is the real, authorized descendant of the Apostles. Christ's message is what moves me. A friend of mine has this beautiful statement framed on his living room wall; it says so many things so well that I'd like to quote it in this book:

> *God Himself, the father and fashioner of all that is, older than the sun or the sky, greater than time and eternity and all the flow of being, is unnameable by any lawgiver, unutterable by any voice, not to be seen by any eye. But we, being unable to apprehend His essence, use the help of sounds and names and pictures, of beaten gold and ivory and silver, of plants and rivers, mountain peaks and torrents, yearning for the knowledge of Him, and in our weakness naming all that is beautiful in the world after His nature—just as happens to earthly lovers. To them the most beautiful sight is the actual lineaments of the beloved. But for the sake of remembrance, they will be happy in the sight of a lyre, a little spear, a chair perhaps, or a place to run—or anything in the world that wakens the memory of the beloved.*

When Maximus of Tyre made this eloquent statement in the first century A.D., he answered forever the narrow criticism of what might be called "religionists"—those for whom the symbols and rituals are more important than the substance of belief. "A chair, perhaps, or a place to run": good symbols for a quarterback who has been through a dozen or more seasons.

Think of the rituals we employ in professional sports: pennants, T-shirts, coin tosses, cheerleaders, drum-roll introductions of the players, "spikes," all sorts of unnecessary additions to the uniform; signals by referees, coaches, and players. Before and after games the fans have developed ceremonies of their own: the tailgate parties, the special Sundays, booing the quarterback (yes, I think a lot of that is pure ceremony). If visitors from outer space descended on one of our stadiums on a fall Sunday afternoon, they might well marvel at the intricacy of this new-fangled religion. If you've ever gone to a football game with someone entirely innocent of the game, you've no doubt found him or her mildly amused at the antics of a good many fans—for whom the last thing to do is follow the action on the field. Yet I'm not trying to put down fans. I'm one of them. Whenever I find myself near Berkeley in the fall, I try to catch a Cal game. And don't think I don't watch Monday night football if we're not playing. There's nothing wrong with rituals; for many people, going to a professional game is simply like going to a parade or a medieval pageant. They want to be part of a crowd, part of an activity, part of *something*. That's very human. Religious ceremonies are very human, too—but they're not the game on the field.

As a latecomer to the realization of Christ's message, I can hardly speak with the wisdom of years. But I want to bear witness, as the least of men in this book, to the power of that message in my own limited experience. I'm not going to be pompous about this; let me put it in terms that George Halas used in a pithy comment he made in his recollection of his building of the Chicago Bears: "If you go out drinking or go out with a babe, it only lasts a few hours. But a win lasts all week." Yes, but even the impossible comeback victories can be savored for only a matter of weeks. What Christ has done for me is to show me how to make an impossible comeback over myself, a victory that has to be won every day but which will last forever.

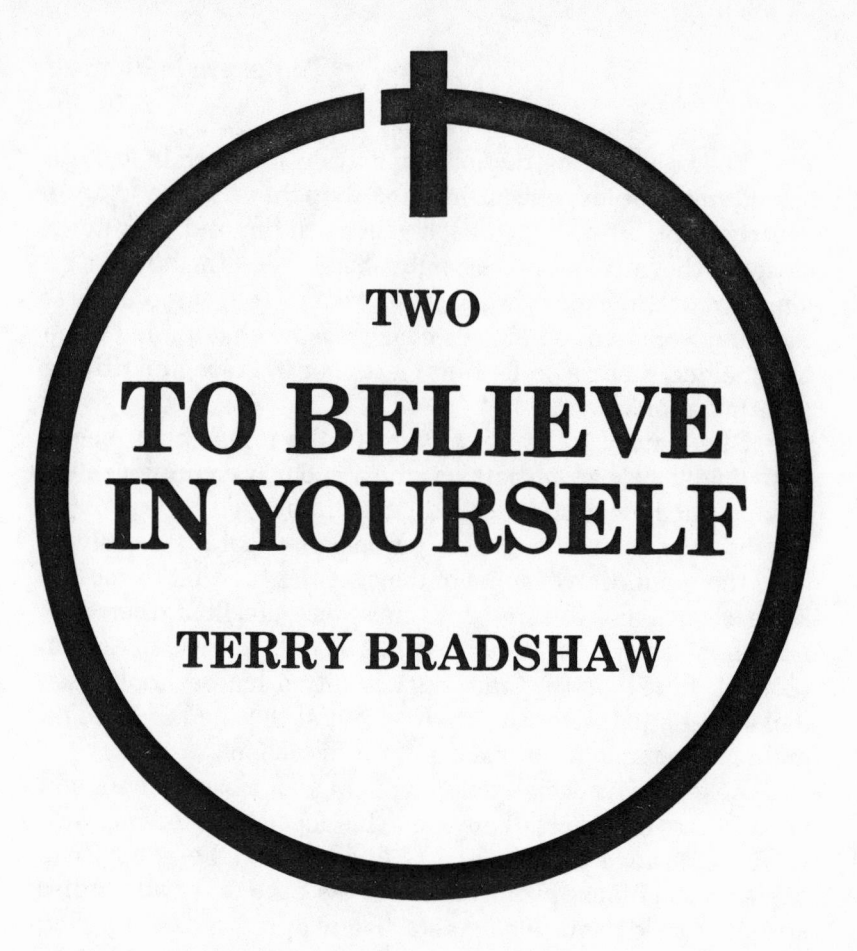

TWO

TO BELIEVE IN YOURSELF

TERRY BRADSHAW

The tall, awkward boy with the funny name stood out obviously from the other freshmen at the track. Ezekial seemed embarrassed by his size. He kept his eyes to himself, as if he had no friends and didn't particularly want any. The new coach, a hurdler in his college days, measured his legs at a glance and made a note to himself.

Slowly, painfully, the boy with the awkward legs learned to stride and breathe and keep his shoulders back. On his third after-school workout he talked to the kid in the locker next to him and told the coach he'd like to try the hurdles. The coach nodded, but kept working on his stride, shortening it from the gangly lope he had first seen, getting the knees higher. Within a few weeks the coach was convinced this was the best hurdle prospect he had encountered in his brief career.

The boy took instructions quickly, as if determined to do something right just once in his life. Keep that right hand up as you clear the hurdle, the coach yelled, and he did. Get down closer to the hurdle. Look straight ahead. Soon the boy was no longer awkward except in the locker room. He entered his first race and won going away. His coach was no champion, but he had molded that raw talent into a runner of grace and driving determination.

One victory followed another in the interschool meets, until finally all that was left was the all-county championships. Zeke, as he now proudly called himself, insisted he was ready for the test, even though his parochial-school league didn't have the reputation of some of the other leagues in the county. Zeke's coach had to agree; his times were excellent, there was no chance he would embarrass his school. In fact, his coach thought, here was that rare opportunity a high school coach looks for—an athlete with such potential that he might go on and make a name for himself and for his school.

Zeke survived his qualifying heat as a close second, and advanced to the finals. If anything, his coach felt more nervous than his protégé as the finalists lined up for the start. Zeke came off the blocks cleanly and was over the first two hurdles stride for stride with the leaders. Then, abruptly, Zeke pulled up short, put his head down, and walked slowly to the sidelines without the suggestion of a limp.

When the coach got to him, he said, "What happened, Zeke?"

"Nuthin'." But there was terror in his eyes.

"Hey, are you OK? Why didn't you keep going?"

"Hell," he said, "I know I can beat those guys."

The coach who told me this story never saw a case like it before or since, but we agreed that the fear of failure is there in the background, even if it's seldom demonstrated as dramatically as in Zeke's case. When coaches say that football or track or any strenuous sport builds character, I think of Ezekial. Every crisis in sports is a test of courage. Saying you can "beat those guys" and actually beating them are two different things. And that's why I think interscholastic sports are excellent: isn't it better to test your courage in a small way, on the playing field, long before the crucial turning points in life?

As Terry Bradshaw readily admits, it took him nine years to go from a first-round draft pick to becoming "an accepted quarterback in the National Football League." I think he's a little too humble in that estimation, when you consider that what he meant by being "accepted" was winning three Super Bowls—and he has now won an unprecedented four. For the six years up to 1980 he dominated the pro game. Yet he considers his friend Roger Staubach, who finished his career at Dallas on a somewhat downbeat note by missing the Super Bowl everybody predicted for him, to be a better quarterback. After Super Bowl XIV, perhaps the best of them all, Terry said, "I think Roger Staubach is being robbed of the opportunity of being recognized as the greatest because he doesn't get to call his own plays like, say, Kenny Stabler does." Terry also ranks Stabler above himself. The humility that seems to gush from "the Li'l Abner of the bayous" is an honest, Christian humility. Yet I think it's a telltale sign that Terry's greatest test of courage was always to trust in his own powers, to believe in himself.

"At the age of thirty-one," he said after Super Bowl XIII, "I think I've learned at least this much, that if I can just tend to the business of being myself, then I can cope with about anything that comes up." He once had to cope with a long interview in *Playboy* magazine, a tough assignment for an unabashed born-again Christian. He felt that Christ would have done the same thing. With the help of modern media—as degrading to women as some of those media may be—he could "witness" his faith to some 22 million readers. And he pulled it off!

It's always tempting to talk about the exploits of a football player on the field when you have a subject like Bradshaw. He can do just about anything a quarterback has to do. Of course he has had unbelievable help, especially in Super Bowl XIV, from two men named Stallworth and Swann. But Terry not only calls his own plays—the only quarterback among the ten playoff teams in 1979 to do so—but makes his own breaks, scrambles, and fights for the extra yard. When he came to discuss me, he typically turned a potential weak point into a paean of praise. "Nobody stays in that pocket like Craig," he concluded. But the Terry Bradshaw I know won his biggest game in the solitude of his own room, during those troubled days when everything that should have been his seemed to be deserting him. And that's what I'd like to talk about.

The Steelers got Bradshaw by the flip of a coin. In the 1969 season they had finished dead last with the Chicago Bears, so there was a toss to see who got the first pick in the draft. For many years Pittsburgh had been a sort of used car lot for quarterbacks—only they sold the good ones and took the clunkers in trade. This time Art Rooney, who, with George Halas of the Bears, is one of the grand old men of the professional game, decided to stick with their young Samson through thick and thin. Shortly before that rookie 1970 season, Terry met Roger Staubach at a Fellowship for Christian Athletes camp in Los Angeles. It was the beginning of a long friendship. Roger had a year of professional experience behind him, but was several years older—his tour of duty in the Navy delayed his entry into the Cowboys' organization. So Roger became something of a Dutch uncle to his future archrival, whereas I came to know Terry first through head-to-head combat, only later through our shared beliefs.

Bradshaw received the royal welcome at Pittsburgh that is the fate of all nationally publicized college stars. He had all the stats and physical equipment, including one of the strongest arms in football history. In high school he had set national records in the javelin throw, which must account for some of that arm strength that has always been a great asset to him. Fans seldom appreciate the purely physical attributes that a quarterback must develop. I know for a fact that weight training is a practical necessity these days for any quarterback who expects to play a full season. Terry had won the Most Valuable Player Award at the Senior Bowl in 1969, and when he signed his pro contract he was invited to the White House to share his thoughts on the game with then President Nixon. No wonder that with all this ballyhoo Terry got the idea that he might take over the number-one job in the first or second year. His disillusionment came early.

Terry's cowboy boots and hat were hardly what the burghers of Steeltown expected of the leader of their local team. Another Terry—Terry Hanratty—was a closer fit to the image of a savvy man about town that the fans idealized as their quarterback. The two rookies got along well with each other, but Bradshaw had to bear the brunt of unthinking criticism because of his country-bumpkin image. When it was also discovered that Bradshaw was a true believer—to use Eric Hoffer's denigrating term—he was a sitting duck for reckless ridicule. Bradshaw liked cattle and Christianity at a time when quarterbacks were supposed to like cocktails and city lights. None of this explains why Bradshaw was erratic in his first few seasons—but it does explain why the uneven results began to get to him. His first—impulsive—marriage, to a former Miss Teenage America in February of 1972, didn't have the roots to sustain it. Yes, Terry was still a Christian through his emotional ups and downs, but he readily admits, even proclaims, that it was verbal Christianity. "I was a phony," he says; "I knew I was a great Christian, but I wasn't acting like one." When I heard this, I thought of Ezekial: "I know I can beat those guys. . . ."

When the 1974 season began, it dawned on Terry that he had to produce soon or lose his job to another rookie. Joe Gilliam was picked up by the Steelers in 1972 as their first black quarterback, and quite a promising one. "Jefferson Street Joe" they called him, a man of great talent and equally great self-confidence. Joe got his chance in the 1974 pre-season, and was unbeaten. Terry sat on the sidelines while the flamboyant rookie won four and tied one of the first six games of the regular season. Bradshaw writes what happened next:

> *I felt like a leper. I wasn't even a part of the team. . . . I came home from practice and sat down in a big chair in my apartment and took a little self-inventory. . . . There were no signs, no messages, no flashes of light, and no bolts of lightning. I wasn't struck blind as Saul of Tarsus was. I just put my head in my hands and began to cry and to tremble all over and finally blurted out, "Here I am, God. I've tried to handle it all by myself and I just can't get the job done. So I'm placing my life in your hands."*

Perhaps it took the trauma of rejection from a football team to bring Terry to his senses, but from that time on football wasn't his god. Nothing mattered, he said, except that he was himself again. The test of that feeling came immediately: he started the following two weeks, then was benched again. This time he rolled with it. His attitude toward himself was one of perfect confidence, because he was no longer alone.

Terry's courage in facing himself can only be described as childlike. For he also had the courage to tell of his conversion without holding anything back. Children know what's going on in the minds of adults, because they themselves are completely without pretense. The biblical injunction comes to mind: "Unless you become as children, you cannot enter the kingdom of heaven." In *The Grapes of Wrath* John Steinbeck paints an unforgettable picture of the two qualities of courage and the ability to sense courage, side by side:

> *Men stood by their fences and looked at the ruined corn, drying fast now, only a little green showing through the film of dust. The men were silent and they did not move often. And the women came out of the houses to stand beside their men—to feel whether this time the men would break. The women studied the men's faces secretly, for the corn could go, as long as something else remained. The children stood near by, drawing figures in the dust with bare toes, and the children sent exploring senses out to see whether the men and women would break. The children peeked at the faces of the men and women, and then drew careful lines in the dust with their toes.*

The large drama of men and women and children fighting for survival in the Great Depression can scarcely be compared with the plight of a football player. Nevertheless, the driving inner torment is the same. Terry Bradshaw did not break. In the act of turning his whole life over to God—an act so childlike in its innocence that it brings only sneers from nonbelievers—Terry says, "I really felt as if someone had lifted a piano from my shoulders. . . . Being a starting quarterback didn't matter. Getting to the Super Bowl didn't matter.

What mattered was that I was myself again and I was determined to stay that way."

It so happened, however, that the Steelers did win their conference championship that year—the first time in forty-two years. They beat Buffalo and Oakland to go to the Super Bowl—number nine. But Terry had played mostly in the later half of the season, whereas in the Steelers' miraculous 1972 season, when they won their first division championship by stealing the playoff game from the Raiders on a last-second tipped pass, Bradshaw had played every game and thrown more than 300 passes. In 1974 he was able to play less than half as much, and had a poorer percentage. Tragically, it was only Joe Gilliam's collapse that gave Terry a chance at all.

Some say that the fans called Terry back—that they wanted a scrambling quarterback who brought back memories of miraculous plays of the previous three years. Others say Pittsburgh wasn't ready for a black quarterback. Behind all the controversy the press remained quiet about the drug habit that was slowly sapping Joe's psyche. He became inconsistent and, faced with the competition from two other ambitious quarterbacks as well as the pressure from unknowing fans, began to lose his nerve. He would struggle through the 1975 season, be released by the Steelers, catch on with the New Orleans Saints, finally fall from sight after a drug arrest and then resurface in a semipro league. In 1979, fighting for a chance to make it back to NFL, he recounted his ordeal:

I was snorting 20 times a day. When a junkie on a needle would get a $25 bag, I'd have to have spoon. It'd cost me $700, $800 a week. I had a big old jar with coke, heroin, and speedballs—carry it with me everywhere I went. After a while a hit didn't bring a high, it just stopped you from feeling sick so you could function. I'd say, "Hey, Joey, this is not you, you're better than this." So I struggled. It whipped my butt ten, 15 times. But I never let it smack me down to where I said, "to hell with it, I ain't gonna try to get on top of it." That's one of the reasons I finally got on top.

The contrast between two types of individuals as distinct as
Joe Gilliam and Terry Bradshaw could hardly be exaggerated.
Bradshaw recalls how one beer knocked him for a loop in a sort
of initiation as a rookie when he first came to Pittsburgh. He
was Mr. Square; his rival was "Jefferson Street." Yet in their
struggles to find themselves ("Hey Joey, this is not you,"
"Terry, do you think you'll foul things up?") they walked a
remarkably parallel course. In one of his moments of self-
victory, Gilliam said of himself, "There's no shammin' of
myself anymore, so I can't sham anybody else." Bradshaw said
of his newfound resolve: "I made up my mind that Terry Bradshaw was going to be a real, sincere, honest, and up-front
human being. . . ." Gilliam went to the Lord for help, too: "I'm
just getting to a level of awareness about myself and faith in
God that has nothing to do with drugs. I'm starting to understand how much I don't know, and how much I'll never know
but have to take on faith. . . ."

Out of this tragic 1974 season came a Super Bowl trip, a
low-key victory over the Minnesota Vikings, and a new Terry
Bradshaw. He had made a promise to God to confess his faith
in him publicly. After the game he turned the traditional locker
room interview into a media event for Jesus Christ—to the
astonishment of skeptical reporters. He told about his dedication of his life to God, about the turnaround in his personal
affairs. But it was no self-righteous performance; only a man
who had discovered complete confidence in himself could
make such a confession on national television. I don't recall
any other time when a human being has spoken more humbly
and openly to so many of his fellowmen.

Terry also knew that the life of a Christian goes on daily;
one national television interview, or even one a week, doesn't
certify a person for a sort of residual sanctity. He writes:

*I was lonely. I knew my personal life was unfulfilled.
Each night I prayed to God to send me a Christian
woman to love.*

The country south of Shreveport, Louisiana, where Terry
Bradshaw grew up, is sparsely settled with sharecroppers'
homes and an occasional sprawling mansion, a relic of the

plantations that once infused the life of the region with grace
and dignity. It's flat country, but wooded and lush in parts,
ideal for small farms. And it's quiet. Thirty minutes from the
city, near a small town named Grand Cane, at the end of a
washboard dirt road is the Circle 12 ranch. Terry has worn
the numeral 12 on his jersey since high school.

Terry bought his first and only home here when he was
still an uncertain quantity on the Steelers' roster, but he has
no trouble keeping up the payments now. It's big enough to be
rightly called a ranch, and when Terry comes here after the
season he says he sucks up every bit of it like a sponge. On
Spring mornings he rises before anyone else is up, sometimes
before the sun, makes himself a pot of coffee, and heads his
Jeep out to one of the farthest corners of his spread. There,
out of sight of the main house, he sits on a small knoll and
begins his day of prayer and thought.

Sometimes he'll read the Bible for a while, sometimes
he'll dream, for prayer to Terry is a cross between hoping and
thinking and caring. Sometimes he'll plan a talk he's going to
give to a group of teenagers in town, or figure what he's going
to do to the barn that day.

Terry's prayer for a Christian woman to love was answered
in a bittersweet love story whose ending is still, I believe, some
way off. Toward the end of the 1973 season, a group of
Steelers took in an ice show that was traveling through Pittsburgh. Terry thought one of the skaters was particularly attractive: a blonde in a green dress. He asked his buddies if
there was any way to meet her. Sure, they told him—we'll
introduce ourselves backstage after the show and after that it's
up to you. When Terry didn't spot the green dress among the
skaters who greeted them, he asked if there was any way he
could meet her. "You mean Jo Jo?" a young woman asked.
"What's your name?" Jo Jo Starbuck was located, and she gave
the rugged-looking guy in the cowboy hat a polite greeting. He
thought everybody in Pittsburgh must know who Terry Bradshaw was—but then he hadn't heard of Starbuck before. He
asked if she would like something to eat. She quickly noticed
all the eyes focused on the two of them and said no, she had a
lot of telephone calls to make.

Terry put the green dress and the name Jo Jo in the back of his mind, and hoped the ice show might come to Pittsburgh again soon. Then the season was over, he was back to his cattle and quarter horses at the Circle 12, and before he knew it the 1974 training camp was opening. It was midway during that fateful season that Terry made his plea to God to meet a Christian woman to love. God helps those who help themselves, he was told, but the tension of that emotionally draining year kept his mind off everything but football. Finally, when Pittsburgh ground down the Vikings in Super Bowl IX at New Orleans, down the river a piece from Shreveport, Bradshaw decided to give it one more try with the girl in the green dress. He located the Ice Capades and left a message for Jo Jo to call him at the Steelers' office. A few days passed and nothing happened. Then Terry made some personal appearances and headed back down for the ranch.

Six months passed and another season was about to begin. The San Diego Chargers were opening in Pittsburgh, a big test right at the start. Bradshaw's mind was again immersed in football, so that when a message came through the Steelers' office that he was to call Jo Jo Starbuck he drew a blank. He asked a buddy if he could place the name, and all he had to do was say "green dress" and Terry scrambled for the nearest phone. Their messages had all gotten crossed, but now the Ice Capades were again in town and Jo Jo wanted to know if Terry would like to see the show; she would leave two tickets in case he'd like to bring a friend. He told her one would be sufficient.

On that first date, after the show, Terry and Jo Jo sat in a pancake house outside Pittsburgh till 4:30 in the morning, talking about God. Jo Jo was as deeply committed to Christianity as Terry had ever been. Less than a year later, in June of 1976, they were married.

For anyone else but Terry Bradshaw, this excursion into the private life of a couple would be either trivial or cheap. Unfortunately, Terry's complete openness with the press also opened up his private troubles and foibles to a gossip-hungry public. Yes, Terry admitted in an interview in a national magazine in 1978, he and Jo Jo were having problems. The fact was

Jo Jo couldn't take the solitude of the ranch and Terry had no hankering for Broadway. But the way they expressed their differences—as openly as if they were talking it over to a marriage counselor—made them seem quite naive to a cynical generation of jet-setters. Or even to the old generation. . . .

Terry admitted to wanting an old-fashioned, male-dominated marriage: "Being Suzy Homemaker wasn't what I expected," said Jo Jo. Terry said, "Where's my wife? Why isn't she with me where she belongs?" Jo Jo said, "I'd be home alone all day fussing for him, and he'd come home at night exhausted and go to sleep. Then I got a few phone calls from people asking me to come perform, so I went off in a flash." She continued: "On opening night on Broadway, everyone sent me flowers and telegrams, but none from Terry." Terry confessed, "When I went to see Jo Jo in the show—well, it just killed me. It killed me because she was enjoying it so much." The more Terry opened up, the more he appeared to be bitter, self-seeking, and possessive. "She can't throw football in my face because it's football that pays for those mink coats, the Mercedes-Benz, the trips around the world. All I ask is more of a return on my investment than I'm getting right now. . . . I just want a full-time wife, that's all. And in the final analysis, I don't think that's too much to ask."

Between the lines of this dialog one could almost hear the interviewers asking, "This is a Christian marriage?" To top it all off, Terry insisted there was everything to hope for: "Just remember: I love this woman, and that's why I'm fighting so hard. . . . What we're trying now is a daily Bible reading on the phone. We talk twice a day, and it's important for me in the morning because I need the send-off."

The crisis in Jo Jo's life is a highly intense version of the career/homemaker clash that is so prevalent in our times. Terry's crisis is almost of the same kind: he can't give up football for at least a few years (he even says he owes it to his teammates, now that he's at his peak, to keep pulling for the Steelers). Yet he wants the life of a family man, too. Terry and Jo Jo are at the top of their fields. Their situation is hardly ordinary, and so their public airing of their problems makes the average couple squirm in frustration: So you two have the best of both worlds, and you're still squabbling! Yet I'd like to ask: Aren't Terry and Jo Jo simply saying out loud those things that most people choose to leave buried—out of pride, out of lack of honesty with themselves? As painful as it is to both of them, their "witness" to their marriage is quite an eye-opener for all of us to ponder, given our own quite different circumstances. As the song says, "The honesty's too much. . . ."

Whenever there's honesty there's also humor. I like especially Jo Jo's on-target descriptions. Speaking of the Circle 12: "After a couple of weeks I go bananas. We're way out in the country, miles from anything—there's no ice, and there's not even a good dance class." On being alone: "I love going out to dinner and talking with friends. Terry doesn't do that. He goes home and he's alone. And then he pouts and sulks and gets angry and jealous. You see, I know what he's going through. When I was with Ice Capades, I did the same thing: I performed, then I went back to an empty hotel room." And now listen to Terry on the real world: "My world is the real world. Sure, I'm used to southern women and the way they treat their men. That's my heritage. My world isn't all Santa Claus and the Easter Bunny and costumes and spotlights and applause." On the ranch: "We came down here after our honeymoon, and I'd get up and go to work, cut hay all day, work the cattle and horses, and come back to the house and she'd be twiddling her thumbs, bored to death." About possible solutions: "Well, you can't split it down the middle and say Terry wants to live in Louisiana and Jo Jo wants to live in California, so let's split the difference and move to Nebraska."

The honesty may be too much, but out of it comes solutions. As Jo Jo sums up: "Neither one of us is getting the things out of our marriage that we thought we would. All we can do is keep working at it. We have to keep praying and hoping. We just have to put ourselves in His hands and trust God to give us the answers we haven't found for ourselves." Whatever happens in the Terry-Jo Jo story, at least we know they tried.

I admire Terry Bradshaw's openness because I know that no one can believe in himself without first coming clean with

himself. Then he'll discover that most of what's holding him
back are illusions about himself. Terry thought when he first
came to the pros that he'd have to be able to tell racy jokes and
swagger a little to be part of the gang. He found himself
stumbling over his own words. He sensed he was the butt of a
lot of jokes. He deeply resented the implication that he was
dumb. They made up gags about him as if he was the embodi-
ment of a new category of Polish jokes: "He couldn't spell 'cat'
if you spotted him the 'c' and the 't'." For a few years he was
defensive about all this. Then he accepted himself exactly for
what he was. In an interview before the great Super Bowl XIII
clash with Dallas, Terry started talking about his faith in the
Lord. The reporter snapped, "We don't want to hear about
that garbage, Terry." Bradshaw looked at him as if to say,
Well, what then? The reporter went on, "Tell us how you in-
tend to handle the flex defense. . . ." Others chided him about
being so square that he never broke a curfew. Terry answered
matter-of-factly: "Everybody in the world should be in bed by
11:00 P.M. anyway." After Super Bowl XIII, the old dumbbell
image looked feeble, indeed.

Bradshaw likes to remind himself of the opening lines of
The Book of Jeremiah when he's kidded about speaking out
for Christ. There the prophet announces how he was chosen
for his work:

> The message of the Lord was: I claimed you for my
> own before you were ever fashioned in your mother's
> womb, before you were born I set you apart for myself.
> I have a prophet's errand for you among the nations.
>
> Alas, Lord God, I said, I am just a child who has never
> learned to speak.
>
> A child? the Lord said. No, I have a mission for you, a
> message to entrust to you. Have no human fears. Am I
> not at your side?

Then God spells out his message, and urges Jeremiah to be
courageous in delivering it:

> Up, then, and gird yourself like a man, and speak out
> the message I give you. Meet them undaunted, and

they will be powerless against you. Today I will make
you as strong as a fortified city, as a pillar of steel, as a
wall of bronze, to meet king, prince, priest, and com-
mon folk throughout the land. They cannot overcome
you, for am I not at your side?

Terry's coach throughout his professional career, Chuck Noll, has been in an excellent position to observe his development as a fully confident person. Noll says, "He no longer limits himself by fear, the fear of not doing something right. You know, fear is a terrible thing. I see it more and more in every activity in which I get involved. . . . When you conquer fear you're euphoric. This is an experience we have to have. We may not even understand what's happening at the time, but that's part of the educational process. We experience things, then later on find out what it's all about. It then becomes a part of us and we take it for granted. That's pretty much what happened with Terry Bradshaw."

Coach Noll understood that Bradshaw could throw with the finest passers in the history of the game; he was "physically better than anyone else I've seen." At the start of the 1978 season Noll felt it was time to push Terry into another gear. He told him, "You've got the ability. You're prepared. The whole idea is now to relax. Go in there and have fun and relax and don't get in your own way." The season took off like a moon shot and the momentum carried on to two of the finest Super Bowl games in the series. Noll: "I think that was when he started believing totally in himself. It was his turning point."

Terry's going to have a bad hitch here and there. At least I *hope* he's human. Who can predict the many possible turns on the field, on the farm, in a marriage? He has held up well physically; some of his opponents kid him about grimacing so much or taking that extra count when he's knocked down, as if he's out. Maybe that's his way of handling pain. Maybe that's part, too, of letting it all hang out. I'm reminded of the great middle-distance and long-distance runner Emil Zatopek, whose facial contortions made one believe he would drop at any moment. But at times Terry speaks so lovingly of his ranch that

I'm sure some day that's where he'll raise his family—or at least, if you read this, Jo Jo, in a place like it. "One of the most thrilling things in the world is the birth of a little calf or a baby horse," he said. Wait till he has a son.

Terry has shown all of us by his persistent witness to Christ how liberating is the childlike acceptance of oneself. I'm sure there are a hundred "sophisticates" for every Terry Bradshaw who fail to be convinced by his example. They will say a football player has very artificial problems, many of his own making. They will say the human mind—pure reason, the scientific method, rational inquiry—is our noblest power, and it should not be abdicated when emotional turmoil engulfs us. They will argue that placing oneself in the hands of God, as Terry did that day in his room when everything looked so desperate, is a childish rather than a childlike act. They will even say that if it *worked* for Bradshaw it doesn't mean that quite a number of other things might not have worked, too. They will say that such an approach may be an emotional purgative, but has little to do with the question of whether or not God exists, whether heaven exists, whether Christ died for us, and all the other basic precepts of Christianity. They will say that what Chuck Noll told him about relaxing was as important as anything Terry ever read in the "good book."

But all of this is just the point of Terry's example. Daily life is an uncharted sea into which we must plunge every day, and no amount of thinking about it can ever take the place of *belief.* This is why, when I think of Bradshaw these last few years, I recall that originally the Steelers were called the Pirates. But this name was in conflict with the baseball team. Naturally, Terry has become known, from the title of his book, as "Man of Steel." For my part, I rather associate him with the hero of an old comic strip—a rugged, blond, good looking young American who took on any danger in the world with an innocent bravado. *Terry and the Pirates.*

THREE

TO BELIEVE
IN LOVE

GLENN CUNNINGHAM

"You can't fool kids. If you love them, they know it instinc-tively." At seventy-one years of age, Glenn Cunningham speaks with the enthusiasm of a youngster; he's been around young people by choice all his life, and things tend to wear off on you. And there are about ten thousand boys and girls, men and women scattered around the country who will carry a little bit of Glenn all their lives: he has worn off on *them.*

Glenn and his wife Ruth still take "hopeless" kids into their home, a little ranch some thirty miles north of Little Rock, Arkansas, as they have done since 1946 when they were first married. But some seven years ago they had to slow down; Ruth was fighting high blood pressure and Glenn was tired of fighting creditors on their Kansas ranch; he was perennially on the verge of bankruptcy. Besides, there was the matter of the Cunninghams' own ten children (by his first marriage Glenn also has two older daughters). The young man in the gospel who observed all the commandments couldn't take Christ's final injunction: "Sell all you have and give it to the poor." The "impossible" ideal of love was too much for him. But there are people like the Cunninghams who have taken Christ quite literally.

Recently I mentioned Glenn Cunningham to a rookie on the Broncos and I drew a blank. "Sorry, I haven't heard of him. Who is he?"

"Before your time," I acknowledged. "From the thirties."

"Oh. What position did he play?"

Well, I'm hardly old enough to have known Glenn in his competitive days, but I did come across his name many times when I was growing up. You can't read about the Olympic Games, and especially that momentous one at Berlin in 1936, without hearing about the Iron Horse from Kansas. He kept one of the best secrets in all sports history for twenty-five years—actually for almost fifty years—concerning the four-minute mile. But the story of his remarkable achievements in track goes back even further, to a bleak winter day in 1917.

Two boys trudged through a Kansas wheat field before dawn to prepare their one-room schoolhouse for their teacher. It was their job to open up, light the wood stove, clear the blackboards. A great civics lesson—or was it politics, economics, or geography?—was then going on in Europe. The newspapers were full of the fiery destruction of the Great War. The older of the two boys, Floyd Cunningham, groped in the darkness for the can of kerosene, doused the kindling in the stove, and struck a match. But someone had replaced the kerosene with gasoline.

In the explosion, Floyd was knocked unconscious and was dead on arrival at the hospital. His eight-year-old brother Glenn was so severely burned that the doctors thought it was only a matter of time for him to follow. They suggested amputating his legs to save his life, but Mrs. Cunningham would not allow it. Six weeks passed; Glenn responded with courage of his own and refused to die. Now skin was grafted onto his painfully twisted legs, and massaged daily by his mother. After six months Glenn was recovered enough to leave the hospital, but it was a year before he could get around under his own power.

In one of those paradoxes of nature that seems hard to describe by any other name but divine providence, it was the burning of Glenn's legs that made them strong. He had to exercise daily to maintain circulation, to compensate for the weakening of some nerves. Soon he was galloping across the wheat fields like a colt, and, in fact, he says that he had a favorite sport: chasing jackrabbits. When he went to high school nothing could keep him from the dirt track etched in a 440-yard orbit around the football field. Perhaps it was a form of compensation, too, that infused Glenn's eagerness to study as well as run. In any case, he resolved to make every possible use of the gift of life that had been given him for the second time by his mother. He wanted desperately to go to college, an aspiration not so easily satisfied by a poor farm boy in the 1920's.

Glenn recalls today that his high school coach was typical of his era—he had no idea of training. "He thought hard work would burn us out. But then, innovative coaches are rare. Most coaches hold back their athletes. This one didn't know anything about track; he was also the baseball and football coach, and his philosophy held everybody back in all three sports." But Glenn had to train just to keep his legs in condition to walk. And, many years before theory caught up with him, he had to learn to stretch and relax his muscles before attempting to work out. Glenn began winning races, especially at the mile distance, from the first day he went out for the team.

One day, as a high school senior some time in the late twenties, Glenn won a race that history has never recorded but which has the significance of winning ten Super Bowls in a row. It was a race with a stopwatch, with only his coach watching. Without competitors breathing down his neck or falling well off the pace, Glenn simply poured it on for all he was worth, for the sheer joy of speed. When he crossed the finish line his coach looked down at the time and saw to his amazement that

Glenn had broken the four-minute mile. "Yes, the stories are true," Glenn says of this unheard-of feat, "I once broke the four-minute mile in a practice time trial. My coach didn't want anyone to know about it. I think he was afraid he'd be accused of child abuse. . . ."

More than twenty-five years later, in May 1954, Roger Bannister would officially go under the four-minute marker. Ten years later, Jim Ryun would be the first high-schooler to break four minutes—officially. Since Glenn never came close to breaking four minutes thereafter—*close* meaning within five seconds—it's possible that the track was incorrectly measured at that little Kansas high school, or that the coach started or stopped the timer incorrectly. Glenn Cunningham is the last person to gloss over these possibilities. For a master's thesis in college he wrote a dissertation on hand-held versus automatic timing devices. Yet Glenn always had an accurate sense of his own running time and he knew the lap times on this particular occasion. "I was sure in my own mind of what I had done," he explains, "and I wasn't looking for recognition. Remember, it was only with the passing of time and the slow progress toward the magic four-minute mark that so much importance was attached to it. I'm thankful now for my coach's attitude. The Lord was good to me in many other ways."

Yes, He was; but Glenn is a walking example of the maxim, "The Lord helps those who help themselves." Paavo Nurmi was the reigning world record holder, with a time in excess of 4:10. A Frenchman by the name of Jules Ladoumegue sliced it down to 4:09.2 in 1931, and then the chase for the magic mark began in earnest. At the Los Angeles Olympics of 1932, three runners emerged as prime candidates: Eric Ny of Sweden, Jack Lovelock of New Zealand, and Cunningham. Glenn missed a medal, coming fourth, but the young man running for the University of Kansas immediately jumped to international attention. The following summer Lovelock entered a major meet at Princeton and knocked 1.5 seconds off the Frenchman's world mark. The indoor mile had meanwhile become popular in America. Cunningham became the third American to hold the world record in this version of the classic, with a clocking of 4.09:8 in early 1933. Because of the tighter turns, well banked or not, an indoor track is generally a second or two slower than the customary 440-yard oval. Cunningham was clearly hot on Lovelock's trail. Eleven months after the New Zealander's record performance, Glenn journeyed to the same track to knock another second off the world standard. It was June 1934, and the American held both the indoor and outdoor mile records.

A certain eerie drama has always hung over the early 1930's, bestowing on those years an emotional importance not felt for any other period in this century. There was the Great Depression, the sobering reality of our own economic fallibility; there was the ominous rise of Nazi Germany, the discovery of a face of evil among nations. Underneath it all there was a feeling of things out of control, and a naive America was finally trying to come of age in an uncertain world. What could be more naive as a symbol of this national trait than a young man who talked about the Scriptures, refused publicity or honors even as he won world titles, and was a living example of Horatio Alger triumph over adversity: the little boy who was told he might never walk again? Glenn Cunningham graduated from the University of Kansas with the highest academic record in his class. Yet to make the Eastern indoor track circuit he had to grab a train on a Wednesday and not return again until the following Monday. That schedule also put a crimp in his working hours, for he had to get in twenty-five hours a week to earn the ten dollars he needed for weekly living expenses. Once he split his princely weekly earnings with a friend to keep him in school. He says about those crowded times: "We learned to make things count. I wouldn't eat on the train—too expensive—but would get a candy bar when we stopped in Chicago. Training, running, working, studying—somehow we worked it all in—because those were our values."

Cunningham lowered his indoor mark in 1934 after one of those foodless train rides, then went on to the University of Iowa's graduate school. He was looking ahead to the Berlin Olympics; he had been able to sandwich in a tour of Germany with other U.S. trackmen after the Los Angeles games. But the more Glenn saw of the world, the more he realized his purpose on earth had something to do with that Kansas schoolhouse where he had had a fiery rebirth into life.

There was no mistaking the direction the world was taking in 1936. As Glenn looks back on it now, he recalls: "I could see a tremendous difference from my first trip to Germany. Anyone who had eyes and ears could see that they were building up for war. I could hear the soldiers miles away, marching in their hobnail boots." Four months before the games, Hitler had invaded the Rhineland, and Europe had backed away from a confrontation. Protests were widespread, but the Olympic fever of athletes and their backers among fans and business firms carried the day. As there are today, there were rationalizations about not mixing politics and sports—as if war was simply a matter of politics. Unlike today, the mid-1930's were also infected with broad racial prejudices that also masqueraded under the veil of politics. Magazine articles previewing the Berlin games noted the number of "Negroes" in critical positions on the American team. Almost forgotten was the dropping of two Jewish sprinters from the American relay team out of deference to the anti-Semitic policies so arrogantly announced by the "host" nation. The hopes of America in track hung mainly on Cunningham and another sensational high school prodigy, Jesse Owens.

There were many similarities between Owens and Cunningham, despite their differences in age and race. At about the time Cunningham was establishing the indoor mile record, Owens was uncorking that great leap of well over twenty-seven feet in the broad jump (now the long jump) that was to remain the world standard until the Olympics at Mexico City in 1968! Owens was also a high schooler when he set that mark. And Owens was as self-effacing as the Iron Horse. He had watched his idol, Charley Paddock, set one record after another ever since the 1920 Olympics; and when he wondered if a black man could aspire to international recognition in track, his coach told him, "Everybody should have a dream." Years later, when he heard Martin Luther King cry, "I have a dream," he knew it was a universal language of courage.

Owens turned out to be unstoppable in the 100-yard dash

and the 220. He would later lead off a record-shattering performance by the Americans in the 440-yard relays. But strangely, in the event in which he held the world record, the broad jump, he was having difficulties qualifying for the finals. This was the event in which he was closely challenged by the German ace, Lutz Long. It was the only real chance for the proponents of the "master race" theory to show up the "American auxiliaries," as the Nazis derisively called the American black athletes at the games. After two jumps, Owens was out of the running for a qualifying place. "I felt suddenly as if my legs couldn't carry even the weight of my body," he said later. He, the world record holder, was going to be shut out even before he had a chance to compete with the German champion.

Then Long walked over from the German contingent, took off his sweatshirt, and placed it next to the takeoff board as a marker. In perfect English he told Owens that he was trying too hard to hit right on the board and would do better if he concentrated on distance. With the sweatshirt as his guide, Owens qualified on his third and final jump. Then, as Hitler and his staff watched in dismay, Owens won the final with a jump second only to his own world record. Lutz Long was second. Owens said later, "Lutz came second, but in my book of sportsmanship he will always rank first."

It was now up to Cunningham to defend *his* world record in the mile. The competition was truly international: the other top finishers from the 1932 Olympics had qualified: Luigi Beccali of Italy, John Cornes of Great Britain, Phil Edwards of Canada, and the strongest, Eric Ny of Sweden. But everyone suspected that it would be a race between Cunningham and the previous world record holder, diminutive Jack Lovelock of New Zealand. In such a strong field, the finishing kick of the American was considered his ace in the hole.

After three of the four laps, everything seemed to be going according to form. Eric Ny was leading, as he had to with his steady style. The muscular Cunningham began to make his move from second place, passing Ny with three hundred yards to go. Almost immediately the frail-looking Lovelock moved up through the pack in what appeared to be a premature burst of speed. Cunningham was losing ground to him, but he hadn't begun his own kick yet, and there was still a quarter of the track ahead. Yet somehow Lovelock had wound himself up, as he remarked afterwards, like a spring, and his finishing kick became stronger as he ran shoulder to shoulder with Cunningham coming out of the final curve. The New Zealander pulled ahead of Cunningham's desperate sprint to finish comfortably six yards in the lead.

Glenn Cunningham came home with a silver medal and a feeling of growing concern for the black athlete in the world, as well as in America. The winner of an unprecedented four gold medals—a feat unmatched to this day—received no welcome from the White House, for Jesse Owens was still simply "Negro" in his own land. The sports pages were the only democratic institution that was color blind. Glenn plunged back into his studies, aiming now for a doctor's degree at New York University. And he began to train even more diligently, with the vision of another chance at Olympic gold four years hence, in 1940. His outdoor mile record was shaved by three tenths of a second by Stanley Wooderson, but Glenn was the master of the indoor track. In March of 1938 he knocked a full four seconds off his own record, stunning the track world.

He began to attract attention as something of a character, even though his natural modesty usually protected him from the press. The trouble was—those scarred legs. As he said recently, "Pinched nerves in my upper back have pained me for sixty years. I feel the pain this minute. The blood in my legs never circulated too well. So, my warmups before a race must have looked funny to a crowd. I'd throw my neck around like a horse and kick my legs like a dancer. People thought I was trying to attract attention and booed. But I didn't care. That's the only way I could run, and win."

He was described as sticking to a wearisome warm-up routine—jogging a full mile before each race. As he went along, his knees were held high like a bicycle rider's. He shook his hands, as though they were asleep, to stimulate circulation, and he moved his head back and forth to loosen up neck muscles. By starting time he was relaxed from head to foot. Glenn was not only well ahead of his time in training techniques; he was also living in a world of pain all his own.

Glenn got his doctorate at NYU, all right, and the press predicted, "More than likely he'll end up as a coach and physical education teacher." Not unexpectedly, however, first peace vanished, in 1939, then the hopes of another Olympics, and finally the expectation of a normal family life. Glenn's indoor mile record would not be broken until 1955—by fellow Kansan Wes Santee; that meant a twenty-two-year span as world champion. But soon enough Glenn was just another swabbie of Uncle Sam's Navy. There would be no chance for a gold medal—not in 1940 or in 1944.

After the war Glenn tried to live up to the expectations of the press by taking over the job of physical education director at Cornell College in Iowa. But the roots of his Kansas farmland kept pulling him back. That's where he belonged; there was something more for him to do in life than direct an athletic program and pursue his own career as a runner or coach. At Cornell College he met Ruth, and between them they decided to tackle a problem they had both grown up with. They had been fortunate enough to make it to college—"but for the grace of God" there were hundreds of other young people who had never made it to high school and yet were just like them. With his GI nest-egg and Ruth's pioneering spirit as their main assets, the Cunninghams bought a ranch that would serve as their own home and as a refuge for deprived or wayward children who had nowhere else to go. Ironically, the ranch was in a little town called Burns, Kansas. It was 1947. Twenty-nine years of hardship lay ahead—and love.

There may be something in the sweep of the Kansas sky, the primordial simplicity of man's dependency on the land and the vagaries of nature, that has drawn the human heart here back to a fundamental kind of religion. This is the Bible Belt, across to Oklahoma and Texas, Arkansas, Kentucky, Tennessee. But in Kansas there seems to have been less of an evangelistic form of Christianity, more of an accommodation with the twentieth century and with the reality of the needs of modern man. Kansans in a sense are Christians in transition.

Away from the farmlands, from the loneliness of the

range, people use the phrase "Bible Belt" derisively, as if to
say, "What, read the Bible? We know better. We're beyond
that." They may talk about "the Bible of the electronics industry" in referring to a book, using the word analogically. But
the real Bible is something your grandmother recorded births
and baptisms and marriages in, something one finds in hotel
rooms under the stationery, something that contains many
poetic and dramatic utterances but with an underlying spirit
that is passé to a scientific mind. Read the Bible? That's for
simpletons.

Novelists have attempted to winnow the sociological data
collected from this vast region as background for their stories,
and their stories have become accommodations between fact
and fiction. Truman Capote's *In Cold Blood* framed the story
of Percy Smith, who was hanged in 1965 in Kansas for the
killing of eight people, against a background of violent child-
hoods, poverty, and a stern, uncompromising social order.
More recently, in *The Executioner's Song,* Norman Mailer
searched for meaning in the tragic life of killer Garry Gilmore.
Again the deeds of the protagonist were measured against the
starkness of his natural surroundings and the helplessness of
one frail human being in the vortex of social change. Violence
and senseless tearing of the fabric of human order are hardly
the private property of the Bible Belt states. But it does seem
that this is the region where the Bible and the bullet live more
compatibly side by side.

The Cunninghams grew up with the Bible, lived on it.
Glenn's mother read it to him in the long hours of massaging
his legs and preparing him to make up his school work. It grew
in importance in his life as he saw more of the world, worked
his way through a Depression-era college education, and experienced a world war. One of the famous passages—from the
first letter of Paul to the Corinthians—is a favorite of Glenn's:

> *Love suffers long and is kind; love does not envy; love*
> *does not parade itself, is not puffed up; does not*
> *behave rudely, does not seek its own, is not provoked,*
> *thinks no evil; does not rejoice in iniquity, but rejoices*
> *in the truth; bears all things, believes all things, hopes*

> *all things, endures all things. Love never fails. But*
> *whether there are prophecies, they will fail; whether*
> *there are eloquent tongues, they will cease; whether*
> *there is knowledge, it will vanish away. . . . And now*
> *there remain faith, hope, and love, these three; but the*
> *greatest of these is love.*

The directness of Paul appealed to Glenn. Arcane theological discussions and religious mysteries, such as the ancient practice of "speaking in tongues," were not his focus. Further along in the same letter, Paul brings up the controversy over "tongues," a sort of mystic God-directed preaching in which the speaker has no control over his choice of words. Paul appeals to straightforwardness: "For if the trumpet makes an uncertain sound, who will prepare himself for battle? So likewise you, unless you speak words easy to understand, how will what you are speaking be known? For you will be speaking in the air." Paul pursues the matter as if to say, "to make myself perfectly clear":

> *There are many kinds of languages in the world, and*
> *none of them is without significance. Therefore, if I do*
> *not know the meaning of a language, I will be a*
> *foreigner to him who speaks it, and he who speaks it*
> *will be a foreigner to me.*

There is nothing mysterious here, and Glenn loved the message. He saw clearly what he could do to practice the Christian message of love. As brilliant as he was academically, he chose to return to his familiar way of life on the farm, in his native Kansas. For he felt an affinity with the lost young people of the world, so many of whom he had seen as he grew up to leave them behind. And some of whom might easily grow up to be Percy Smiths or Garry Gilmores. . . .

Christian love, as expressed in the basic injunction to love one's neighbor as oneself, suffers in interpretation because of the many uses of the word "love" we so readily employ. It's not difficult to love one's friends, one's husband or wife. Physical, sexual love . . . why not?! We also speak of the love of children, of pets, of familiar surroundings. We love contemporary heroes in sports, politics, or even war. Less easily we love great figures from the past, for immediacy seems critical to this kind of love. All of these forms of love may be more readily understood if we use more precise words for them: lust, self-gratification, fondness, admiration. But Christian love does not feed on something else, "does not seek its own." Rather, it grows from one's own capacity to care. Christian love is a sort of self-awareness.

When Glenn and Ruth first sent word around that they were willing to take in unwanted boys and girls at their ranch, the reaction was guarded. Some local courts turned over "hopeless" cases to them—boys who were continually in and out of reform school. Others drifted by, unwanted anywhere else. Glenn recalls:

> *The story was almost always the same—they had been rejected by a mother or father. One little tot was hardened with cynicism. His mother had dumped him at bus stations, but he kept coming back like a dog. He learned to grow up with animals in a lean-to out back, because that's how he saw himself. At first he fought us, too, because we were the uncaring parents in his mind. And we were firm with him, though it broke our hearts, because in the end love always shows through firmness.*

The Cunninghams refused to take any public funds, insisting that parents or near relatives contribute to the ranch of their own free will. Even today, Glenn declines the calls of welfare people, even though he could qualify for federal funds. He has always felt that welfare is counterproductive, or at least doesn't work in his type of operation. Inevitably, the contributions were sparse, for in most cases the parents were too hardened to be concerned if their children lived or died. Over the first sixteen years of running his ranch, Glenn says that he averaged sixty-eight dollars a year in contributions. The rest came from his family's and his young charges' efforts at farming and raising animals.

In the first few years of their grand experiment, the Cunninghams were alternately overwhelmed and deserted by children, like a sand castle on the shore of an ocean. During their first summer they somehow managed to take in some six hundred boys and a few girls. Many would soon run away, unable to handle the strict discipline the ranch required. But they had to choose to stay or leave. Once, a rambunctious young man refused to do his chores. Glenn laid down the rule that he had to give to everyone: "Do your work or you don't do anything else around here." The boy insisted it wasn't fair, packed up his few things, and walked away. Fifteen years later he returned to report that this was the best lesson he had ever learned. "I needed a strong hand over me, and I didn't know it," he said.

In his insistence on hard work, firm discipline, voluntary contributions, and freedom to come or go, Glenn Cunningham fits the image of the old-fashioned taskmaster; "yes, you can say I favor the old values," he concludes. But he also has a rationale for his rules that goes deep into the human psyche; he's the last person to love authority just for the sake of authority. Consider his attitude toward punishing: "I believe a good tanning if deserved doesn't hurt." In the great philosophic tradition that goes back to Plato, this theory can also be expressed in terms of the child's inherent sense of justice. When wrong, nothing a child can do will ultimately be as important as paying for his wrongs. "Many a child on the ranch has wiped the tears and come back to thank us."

Or consider the theory of Cunningham's that he calls "animal therapy." The rejected child is afraid of all adults, needs to learn—somewhere, somehow—that all adults are not the same forbidding authority figures. Every child also needs responsibility, something to take charge of. These two needs were dealt with at one stroke by Glenn's practice of matching kids up with farm animals. "Each one was given an animal, usually a horse, to 'own' and care for. In one of our early years we had eighty-eight kids and eighty-eight animals. Kids get along with animals. They go defensive with adults." Old fashioned?

The financial burdens of running a ranch so vulnerable to untimely demands kept the Cunninghams in a sort of poverty most of the time. They cut back on everything that wasn't geared to survival; over one five-year period they had no car,

so they made trips to town for shopping by foot or on horse-
back. When creditors pushed them to the wall, they managed
to come up with ideas to raise a little money—such as charging
one dollar per family to visit their "Wild Animal Farm," which
grew to include llamas, water buffalo, and monkeys. When that
grew stale, they opened the farm up free, just to get people
interested in their enterprise. They had none of the promo-
tional flair of places like Father Flanagan's Boys' Town, yet
they survived.

But in 1960 they were forced to sell the Burns ranch and
move to a smaller spread, at Augusta, Kansas. By the middle
of the decade, when they celebrated twenty years in the
business of awakening love, they could estimate that some ten
thousand children, primarily boys, had at one time or another
been their guests. Not all, by any means, stayed very long; not
all broke the pattern of their early rejection from the world of
adults. Some went back to drugs, alcohol or both; some turned
to violence. But judges of juvenile courts and social workers
and surprised parents tagged Glenn Cunningham with a label:
"the man of ten thousand miracles."

Glenn Cunningham's third oldest son is a pastor in a
Bible church not too far from where the "ranch" now is in
Arkansas. Most of the children have grown and gone—some
are in college—and so Glenn and "the missus" now have a
chance to devote more time to their own lives. In particular,
Glenn likes to exchange ideas with his minister-son, whose
training is in Hebrew and Greek as the basis for his study of
the Bible.

Pastor Cunningham is accustomed to spending eight
hours delving through books to research the theme of a Sunday
morning sermon. He is the type of scholar-preacher who has
brought much respect back to the study of the Bible in recent
years. Instead of quoting blindly, often mistakenly because of
the changing meaning of words, Christians like the Cunninghams now have a firmer grip on the meaning of their faith; in
particular, they are no longer misled into interdenominational
divisions by confusing too-literal passages concerning the

organizational church. Those who live by the sword die by the sword, and those who live by literalness in biblical quotations will see their faith die in a tangle of contradictions. The central message of Christianity, as expressed in that complex word "love," is simplicity itself.

Glenn points out that his favorite passage from St. Paul, in a letter to the Corinthians, quoted earlier, was often garbled in the minds of devout believers because the word "charity" was used instead of "love." Chapter 13 begins:

> *Though I speak with the tongues of men and of angels, but have not love, I have become as sounding brass or a clanging symbol. And though I have the gift of prophecy, and understand all mysteries and all knowledge, and though I have all faith, so that I could move mountains, but have not love, I am nothing.*

If you replace "love" with "charity" in the places where it appears here, the whole thing sounds like an appeal for larger contributions when the basket is passed! But "charity" was a literal translation from the Latin *caritas*, which meant a sort of unselfish love; the word "caring" comes from the same root. And here I can't help but think of what Roger Staubach wrote once: "Christianity seems to me to come down to caring for other people."

So it also happens that some of the immediate concerns of the early Christians cannot be translated literally to our modern milieu. In the familiar Christian wedding ceremony, wives were admonished to "love, honor, and obey" their husbands, but nowadays the "obey" has been omitted or tactfully changed to "cherish." St. Paul is often accused of being the first Christian macho because of quotations like this. Yet in the social context in which he wrote, "obeying" might well have been something of a practical necessity. So we have to translate not only the words but the spirit in which they were intended to be taken.

Not all of us have the inclination or the aptitude to be biblical scholars, but there's nothing to prevent a full and wide-ranging discussion of the symbols and meanings we see in our faith. I was reminded of this when former heavyweight champion George Foreman made his debut as a minister to prisoners.

After preaching to and baptizing twenty inmates of San Quentin prison, in California, he was quizzed by the press about the possibility of his returning to the ring. He said, "I've been offered $5 million in package deals to come back. I've been contacted by Don King, who told me he had a robe for me, with a cross on it, if I came back. I told him, 'Don, what's the matter with you! Jesus ain't a cross. Jesus is love!' " Others might quarrel with this neat formulation, recalling that Christ also said that we should take up our crosses daily and follow Him. But the spirit of Foreman's interpretation is right on target, in my opinion: Christ isn't the cross—He makes *your* crosses easier to bear because of love.

There are as many ways of "witnessing" one's faith to others as there are human personalities. George Foreman may do it in the ring, or at a mass baptism of prisoners. Johnny Cash has chosen to do it at San Quentin also, with a series of memorable concerts combining pure entertainment with a man-to-man message of hope. He knows what it's like to be there. Even in Las Vegas, at headliner shows, at least one star entertainer has chosen to leave a Christian message along with his very worldly musical presentations. Bobby Vinton frequently saves a religious song, "He," for the climax of his act. His Las Vegas audiences are no Bible Belters, but they are struck in their own way by this eloquent message.

Glenn Cunningham now also has, in his semiretirement, more time to formulate the reasons why he plunged into the task of rescuing cast-off children some thirty-five years ago— with complete abandon. Why? He's not a strange bird, a saint or a sinner. Though he is this nation's greatest living distance runner, he's not overawed by the running boom. If he's called to help promote a worthy cause—the saving of a park, the betterment of a recreation program—he'll go. He'll give press interviews, lead a jogging session, jostle the memories of middle-aged reporters about the great moments of sports history of the twenties and thirties. He'll tell you point-blank what he thinks: that people need to be sensible about running, and not feel anxious if their friends are caught up in the running craze. He'll preach moderation, this man who has always pushed himself to the limit of his sport. He knows the cost, and the reason. Mainly, he says it's a matter of dollars and cents, except that the dollars and cents are those invested in human beings; he says the greatest asset of the country is young people, and the cost of neglect of this asset is too high. The cost of neglect. . . .

This may be the reason why there are Glenn Cunninghams, the people who do what seems impossible. Glenn wouldn't admit that what he attempted was impossible; he would say it was just his life. But people like Glenn calculate the human cost, as they have learned that cost in their own lives. This is why Glenn's kind of love is no mushy, sentimental love—it is a discovery of something within himself, rather than an indulgence in something outside himself.

Glenn likes to say that love is, above all, a free spirit. You don't have to kill people by insisting that they prove to you they love you. Love will prove itself. It will shine through all disguises. It may help if a husband says to his wife, "I love you," over the kitchen stove, especially if he is afraid to say "I love you" except when he's making love to her. But "love does not parade itself." It is so interwoven in nature, in patient looks, in simple sharing of the goods of life, that no one need demand it to be expressed to him or her. Glenn, you are for every living athlete a vision of a complete human being. I love you.

If men and women are to make progress in human relations as well as in technology, if they are to develop at long last into nonviolent, caring beings as much as they have become tinkerers, farmers, and builders, then the lever they need is nothing short of love. We do not seem as yet to have the kind of courage to love that people like Albert Schweitzer, Mother Theresa, or Glenn Cunningham have shown, each in his or her own way. The challenge is there, as expressed by the mystic theologian Teilhard de Chardin:

> Someday, after we have mastered the winds and the waves, the tides, and gravity, we will harness for God the energies of love, and then for the second time in the history of the world man will have discovered fire.

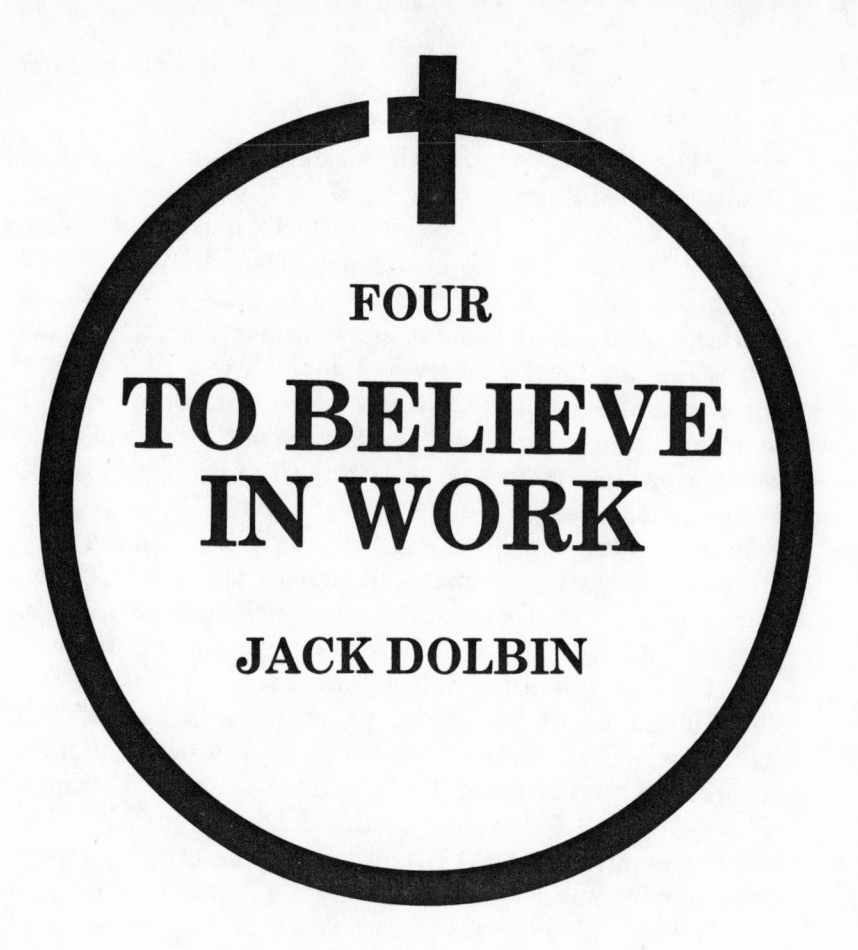

FOUR

TO BELIEVE
IN WORK

JACK DOLBIN

On December 13, 1970, twenty inches of snow fell in New England, but they don't cancel football games for a blizzard. The next day, on a high school field in Hartford, Connecticut, two football teams tiptoed gingerly across the ice to await the playing of the national anthem and the start of a championship game. It was Pottstown, Pennsylvania vs. Hartford for the title of the Atlantic Coast Football League. Most of the players had abandoned their cleats for sneakers, not relishing the prospect of hitting the glass-hard surface all afternoon. In the near-zero temperatures of the morning, the doors of the portable toilets had frozen shut and icicles hung from the shower nozzles. A handful of well-bundled-up fans waited impatiently for the festivities to begin, but the public address system had broken

down. The teams lined up for the kickoff without benefit of the
"Star Spangled Banner."

The Firebirds from Pottstown struck quickly, with King
Corcoran throwing to Ron Holliday, Don Alley, and Jack
Dolbin almost at will. Running backs John Land and Claude
Watts skidded and pushed for short yardage when the passing
attack bogged down. As they had done all year, this team of
eager kids and has-beens trying to make it back to the NFL
knuckled down to their jobs as if they were on the road to the
Super Bowl, piling up a 31–0 victory. In a drafty, makeshift
locker room, coaches Ron Waller and Dave DiFilippo were
handed the league trophy, and there were tears on the mud-
smeared cheeks of veterans and rookies alike. A few beers
were popped, and the victors slapped each other on the back
with frozen hands. Then it was back on the bus to Pottstown.

The Firebirds ordered championship rings for their heroes.
Jack Dolbin recalls, "But to get the rings they told us we first
had to sell fifty tickets at one dollar each to the Pottstown
Awards Banquet that year. I only sold five tickets but I wanted
the ring so bad I bought the other forty-five myself." Two
months later, the year-old Firebirds were dissolved, and thirty
guys found themselves looking for another place to play.

Dolbin hadn't figured this would be the way his boyhood
dreams would end. There had never been any doubt in his
mind that there was a place for him in football immortality. He
was from a long line of athletes, the Dolbins. His grandfather
held the world record in the 100-yard dash in 1916, a respectable 9.6 seconds in the days before starting blocks and cinder
tracks. His father set the broad-jump mark at high school in
Pottsville, a small town about sixty miles north of Pottstown.
Thirty years later, Jack would break his father's record. And
Jack would be courted by dozens of colleges in his senior year
in high school, even though he broke his leg in a Pennsylvania-
Texas all-star game. He was strongly tempted by the lure of the
football powerhouse at Syracuse, but decided in favor of Wake
Forest and its warmer clime. There was a tradition in the coal-
mining country of making a name in football in the South.

The only thing that happened to him at Wake Forest,

Jack recalls, was that he met a young woman there whom he would marry upon graduation and who would change his life with her commitment to a Christian belief. Jack's grandmother was a minister's daughter, and there was always a churchgoing sentiment in the family, but at this stage of his life Jack was concerned only with football. He sustained serious injuries every year at Wake Forest, finally managing to complete about ten games in four seasons. In his last year, Wake Forest was 1–9 and, brilliant though he was as a running back, Jack failed to make the NFL draft.

He returned to Pottsville with a wife, a BS degree in biology, and a gloomy prospect for a job. His father urged him to follow him into the field of medicine as a chiropractor. At five foot ten and 170 pounds, Jack wasn't considered big enough to be a running back in the pros, but his speed caught the eye of a Pittsburgh Steelers' scout. He was offered a contract as a free agent to try out as a defensive back. If he made the team, he would receive $13,000—a reasonable salary for 1970. Coming off a series of injuries, however, Jack felt he had a better chance to prove himself in the minor leagues—and the nearby Pottstown team could use him. Today, ten years later, he admits he was terrified by the challenge of the Steelers, of going up against fifty other guys who were prepared to make hamburger out of him if it took that to make the roster. Jack didn't want to go back to school, either. So he blocked out his fear of failure and signed with the Firebirds for a $500 bonus. They would pay him $150 a game and get him a job as a carpenter's apprentice that paid $85.90 a week.

Jack and Jane set up housekeeping with a TV set, a bed, and some cinder blocks he brought home from work for chairs. "We put the TV set on an orange crate," he remembers. "I'd work in the morning and practice football at night. I didn't discover how tough it was for Jane until I came across some letters she'd written her mother. It broke my heart to learn of her despair. The thing that made it bearable for her was her faith in Christ." It was bearable for Jack because his team was the class of the league, and the dream of being snapped up by the NFL in a glamor position drove him like the furies. With the Firebirds he would learn how to play wide receiver, where he could use his speed and quick hands. Then they would come to him.

The first and only season for the Firebirds began with an eight-hour bus ride to Roanoke, Virginia, and ended on that frozen field in Hartford. "That bus ride seemed like eight days," Jack says. "We tried to play cards going down but everybody was edgy and restless. After we beat them by a huge score, 41–0, you might think the ride back would have been better. But I can't describe the frustration of sitting there, bruised up, hurting all over, trying to sleep while the guy behind me had his stereo turned up full blast." When they played at home, on the Pottstown high school field, they had to shower in shifts to make the four nozzles go around. They dressed in hallways, in locker rooms with two inches of water on the floor, in utility rooms where they had to dodge steam pipes and where there wasn't room to tie their shoes. The veterans gave the baby-faced kids a preview of where they might be in a dozen years. But it was football, and they had been up there and were willing to go through this to make it again.

When the Firebirds were told to scatter after the 1970 season, offers came in for a lucky few. Jack was one of them: the San Diego Chargers matched the offer he had turned down a year earlier from Pittsburgh. But again it meant facing an uphill battle in training camp. And Jack had given up carpentry for selling life insurance, and seemed to be off to a good start. The New York Giants opened the door for a tryout, too, but Jack was now convinced that he couldn't afford to come home as an also-ran. He dropped hints that he was still injured.

When summer came around, however, the idea of being a working stiff for the rest of his life panicked him. He had to stay in football, some way, any way. He heard a team was forming a few miles up the road in St. Clair, under the devastating name, the Schuylkill County Coal Crackers. Though most of the competing teams were in southern Pennsylvania and Maryland, there were exotic entrants from Cumberland

(the Colts), Norfolk (the Neptunes), and Orlando (the Pan-
thers). Jack hauled his old gym bag up to St. Clair, population
5,000, and made the team. It was easier than New York.

After several depressing months of playing to a gallery of
miners lining the coal banks, the team was mercifully dis-
banded. The insurance business had also soured for him. The
dream of making a career in football shattered, Jack fell back
on his father's advice and enrolled in chiropractic college in a
suburb of Chicago. At nights he worked as a detective for a JC
Penney store, chasing shoplifters instead of footballs. Classes
and work went well, but one evening he returned to his dismal
apartment in a factory section of the city to be told by Jane
that a baby was on the way. This was the breaking point: years
of college ahead, a barely adequate salary, and another mouth
to feed. "It was a very emotional time," Jack says; "I felt I'd
made a mess of my life."

All through college Jack had dormed a few feet from the
chapel, and had never set foot in it. Jane had remained devout
in spite of Jack's indifference; but now a dramatic change
came over him. One evening he found himself daydreaming as
he peered through his binoculars at his observation post at the
store. Suddenly, spontaneously, his eyes filled with tears: "I
did something very unnatural for me: I got on my knees and
prayed. I asked forgiveness, asked Jesus to enter my life and
save me." When he stood up he felt confident that something
would happen, that his prayers would be answered.

When Jack and Jane talk about those days in Chicago,
they can now see that it wasn't the emergence of the World
Football League, in 1974, that gave Jack his chance, but *how
he faced it.* It makes a nice story that a few days after Jack got
down on his knees someone called out of the blue to offer him a
tryout with a new professional team in Chicago. Yes, the newly
formed Chicago Fire laid out an attractive one-year contract
before the Dolbins, and with a baby on the way it was difficult
to pass up. But the Fire didn't seem too far removed from the
Firebirds, and in his Pottstown mentality Jack would have
backed away from this challenge, as he had earlier, to avoid
trying out for the Chargers, the Giants, and the Steelers. The

difference this time was his acceptance of Christ: he no longer had anything to fear when he knew that Christ would be with him no matter what work he undertook.

He quickly found his work was cut out for him. To induce prospects to come to camp, team representatives are known to minimize the competition. There would be only four or five receivers there, they told him, and "none of them could outrun the shade of a small tree," as Jack put it. Instead, there were fifteen or twenty, including former All-Americans Jim Seymour, Bruce Jankowski, and Todd Snyder, and several NFL veterans. Jack's old knee injury also gave him trouble, but he squeaked by the physical and dug in for six weeks of training. He had no more money for chiropractic school, and if he could make the grade for a year he might be able to save enough to go back. Just before camp convened, Jane delivered a baby boy.

When the first season of the WFL opened, the Fire had Jimmy Scott at one end and Jack Dolbin at the other. Not only did Jack make the cut, he quickly returned to form, catching fifty-four passes, seven of them for touchdowns, and running up almost one thousand yards. He was in line for a bonus when the league folded as suddenly as it had come on the scene. Many teams of the WFL failed to meet their payrolls; the party was over.

As the Spring of 1975 rolled around, the Dolbins were caught with bigger bills and again nowhere to go. They had a home in the suburbs, heavily mortgaged, baby Josh, and creditors who didn't understand things about football teams not meeting their payrolls. Jack recalls that he was sure something would turn things around, because he had dedicated his work to Christ. But when it finally happened, it was a stunner. Jane greeted him on his return from a day's job-hunting with an innocent question: "Do you know a John Ralston?" Jack tried to think of someone at the local pizza place he owed money to, but the phone number she handed him had a Denver area code. The Broncos were interested in him.

It turned out that several other NFL teams came after him, once it was discovered that the Fire had reneged on his contract and he was eligible. But the Fire's coach, Steve Tensi, had once played for Denver and went out of his way to convince both the Broncos and Jack that they were made for each other. After five years of surviving the rigors of north-eastern cities, Jack agreed that the living might be better in the Mile-High City. A former Florida State quarterback, Tensi was convincing both about living conditions and wide receivers.

Three years later, I was throwing passes to Jack in Super Bowl XII.

In Jack Dolbin's outer office in northwest Denver, patients are greeted by a soft-spoken, thoughtful woman who eschews the usual starched white uniform of a nurse or dental assistant. She is Jack's mother, office assistant, secretary, and loving critic. Critic, because she is politely skeptical of born-again Christians. When she talks about the Bible, she brings to mind Christ's advice about not being lukewarm: "If you are neither hot nor cold I will spew you from my mouth."

"I can't take the Bible literally," she says. "You might say I'm an agnostic, but not an atheist. I think it's just too big for us to figure out. I don't go along with all that gobbledegook." She explains that she's lived in and out of the Baptist Church all her life, but has never felt the personal commitment to Christ the way her son has. "The best thing that ever hap-pened to Jack was Jane. She is the complete wife. And she's always been so deeply religious that it was inevitable that Jack became committed, too."

It's no accident that almost every instance of a dedicated Christian athlete I know of includes a strong, committed woman. Jack Dolbin speaks of *events* as being the language of God. And there is no more riveting event than the coming together of a man and a woman. The women I'm thinking of aren't reformers who set out to make their men over to their own specifications. But the lives of their men were incomplete until the men came to see something unique in their wives.

Some Christians profess to have a more direct communi-cation with God, a more striking and obvious "conversion" than Jack Dolbin's falling on his knees in desperation. Mar-garet Court, Australia's contribution to the world of women's

tennis, experienced a vision of the Blessed Virgin that was a
turning point in her personal life. Others hear voices, or speak
in tongues. But the Christians I know, like Jack, hear God's
voice through the ordinary events of life—sometimes in moments of crisis, often in their workaday world.

Becoming a chiropractor, after that long struggle in
Chicago and the setback of the World Football League, is an
event that has taught Jack more than anything else about the
nature of his faith, as I see it. As a healer himself, Jack has
become quite literally like Christ—but hold the discussion of
miracles, please! Jack's difficult struggle to make his way in
the world, starting as a carpenter, also reminds me of the
Christ who did not feel it beneath him to work at his father's
trade, or to feel compassionate toward fishermen who struggled
all night without making a catch. The dignity of labor is never
preached in the gospels—it is lived; virtually every parable
involves the workaday world of Christ's time, from planting
vineyards to tending flocks to sweeping kitchen floors for lost
coins.

Even soldiers are told in the gospel to perform their
duties faithfully, then practice the doctrine of love in their
private lives. Christ seems especially fond of people who have
to struggle to see Him. On one occasion a cripple has his
friends lower him on ropes through the opening in the roof of a
building. Christ is impressed, refuses to have the man dismissed as a trespasser, and heals him. Like determined auto-
graph seekers, the weak and the strong, the powerful and the
penniless find a way to place themselves before Christ. And He
is especially impressed with the one leper who took the trouble
to return to thank Him for being healed. On Dr. Dolbin's wall is
this quotation:

> The doctor of the future will give no medicine, but will
> interest his patients in the care of the human frame, in
> diet, and in the cause and prevention of disease.

The person who works for his health receives its benefits as
literally as those who worked to receive Christ's blessing.

Jack's profession has not been wasted on the Denver
Broncos. A sort of unofficial team doctor, he was called upon to

find the causes of those mysterious aches, strained backs, pulled muscles, and bruised bones that are everyday occurrences on a football team. There is no competition in his mind between his chiropractic approach and conventional medicine: they are both adjuncts of the healing art. I well remember that painful week before our American Conference championship game against Oakland in 1977. My hip was badly bruised and swollen. It seemed impossible that I'd be able to suit up. Jack worked on it two days before the game, but Red Miller was skeptical—he had seen too many injuries of this kind. Just before game time, without benefit of needles or pills, I struggled into my gear and warmed up. I think I was as surprised as anyone when I told Coach Miller that I was ready to go and did.

Long before Jack got his degree, when he was running out of funds for his tuition in Chicago, he and Jane decided that their baby would be born by natural childbirth. They went to classes together, practicing deep breathing techniques and the exercises that would help Jane deliver her child without anesthetics. They prepared to have the baby at home, with Jack assisting in the obstetrics. But as the time came for Jack to leave for training camp and his big shot at the Chicago Fire, the baby was long overdue. Finally, forty-eight hours before he had to report, two weeks late, Josh arrived. Everything went perfectly. But that, too, was an act of faith that some of Jack's friends and relatives couldn't understand: aren't babies supposed to be delivered in the hospital?

When Jack and Jane talk about marriage and the changing roles of husband and wife in our society, they present the same sort of contrast between traditional concepts and the new ideas of a younger generation. Jack says that women are "liberated in Christ," but Jane sees her career in raising her family, with all the old-fashioned virtues of being a good housekeeper that this implies. St. Paul's advice, that wives should be subject to their husbands, is followed immediately by the admonition that husbands should love their wives as "Christ loves His church." Two thousand years after this prescription was given—after periods of polygamy, chivalry, and Victorian hypocrisy—it's easy to forget that Paul's advice was revolutionary for its time. In his letters to various fledgling Christian communities, Paul was a sort of Dear Abby who had to combine practical wisdom with Christian principles. So when Jack says that women are liberated in Christ, he means they were given an equality in all of Christ's actions that was ahead of its time and is still valid. All of the women in the gospels—Ann, Mary, Mary Magdalen, Martha, the woman taken in adultery, the woman at the well—are strong figures. Only women remain at the cross, and women are the first to discover that Christ has risen. And if Paul appears at times to treat women as a source of temptation to men, adversaries rather than helpmates and equals, his other great confession should be remembered: "I am not all that I should be."

In his successful years with the Denver Broncos, Dr. Dolbin has had to continue to work hard to do justice to both his religion and his profession—in a sport inimical to both. Knowing that his previous lifestyle was "not all that it should be," he has had to avoid the hypocrisy of looking down on his former friends while professing his commitment to Christ. Football constantly holds out prizes to the ego, to jump back on the fast track of adulation and self-congratulation. And friends wonder how a man who believes in turning the other cheek can revel in a game in which most players believe in turning the other elbow instead.

Jack has thought a lot about walking this tightrope of theory and practice. "The image that people take away from a casual reading of the gospels," he says, "is that Christians are meek, and take it on the chin like lambs led to the slaughter. These are images that come from a very superficial glimpse of Christ's teachings." He points out that the word "meek" in such lines as "The meek shall inherit the earth" is a poor translation of the original Greek; more accurately, what is called *meekness* is supposed to be *strength under control.* That's quite a different thing from the Caspar Milquetoast picture of the ideal Christian. On the other hand, it doesn't mean an eye for an eye and a tooth for a tooth—the prescription of the Old Testament. In Jack's second year with the Broncos—before I arrived—the NFL was going through one of those periods of what I call "publicity violence." If the fans get excited by grudges and wild melees on the field, there are always people around who say "Give it to 'em." Pete Rozelle had to step in and discipline several defensive backs for late hits. In an early game with Kansas City, Jack took a difficult pass and had his legs shoestringed out from under him. Tim Gray came in late and got his elbow on Jack's chin as he lay on the ground. His jaw was broken. In the fourth quarter, with the game still undecided, Jack asked for a big mouthpiece and a tight chinstrap and went back in. Going straight at Gray, he beat him one-on-one for a touchdown. "That's the best way to handle a cheap-shot artist," Jack said, but most players would prefer to return the compliment to the jaw.

Wide receivers are the most injury-prone players in the game. The good doctor has had his nose broken every year since 1970, but he doesn't count broken noses any more. His broken jaw didn't prevent him from playing out the season. But his bad knee is another matter. In our 1979 thriller against Seattle, Jack was sidelined before I got into the game. The docs tried to do what is called an arthroscopy on his knee, but the scope couldn't get past the bone chips and arthritic growth that had accumulated there. They operated to remove them, hoping he'd be back after four or five weeks. But he was lost for the rest of the season. Eventually, his knee injury forced him out of active competition for good.

Jack isn't the type of guy to go down without a fight. After all, his very first play as a Bronco should have started him thinking again about Pottstown. It was the first preseason game of 1975. With his great speed, Jack was being tried out on the special teams. He took the opening kickoff and boomed straight up the middle into the defensive wedge; he was carried off the field with a broken nose and a concussion. The next day he showed up for practice to prove what he could do as a receiver: he made the team.

It's disarming to hear such a man speak softly and firmly about a favorite passage of his that begins, "For God so loved the world. . . ." It's then that I realize why Jack has always believed in hard work, and why it's a key to his life: he's a per-sonification of strength under control. When he's invited to speak to boosters' clubs or medical meetings or schools, his

manner is enough to demonstrate what that strength is. Without a lifetime of struggle, without a continuing dedication to
work in the service of his fellowman, Jack could not be the
person he is. It's curious that two actresses recently put their
finger on the same thing. Both Lauren Bacall and Bette Davis,
in separate interviews, said that the one value in their lives
that kept them happy and interested in life was work. Not
lounging around a swimming pool or jetting across the Atlantic, but reading scripts and working for good causes and
doing what they've always done in the field of acting.

"They invite us out to speak for all the wrong reasons,"
Jack says, "but when I get the chance I tell them about my
commitment to the Lord. The fact is, most people are pleased
to hear what's honestly on my mind than another recording of
the standard publicity interview." I've gone through a similar
experience, especially in that Super Bowl year of 1977. We
were facing a showdown game with Baltimore, which was also
9–1. Coach Miller asked the captains to give a short pep talk
before the game. I had nothing rah-rah to say, so I simply told
the rest of the players about my recent commitment to Christ
and what it meant to my own equanimity. Jack told me later
that it mirrored his own mind. But I had to stifle a lot of old
fears to do it. After the Pittsburgh game that year, instead of
the usual locker-room interview that can be taped and played
back on any occasion, I again gave credit to the Lord for our
victory. This was on national television, so I got a lot of flack
about goodie-goodie guys in the NFL who use God as a secret
weapon. Some commentators asked pointedly what I might do
if we lost the Super Bowl. I did the same thing—giving credit
to the Lord for what we were able to accomplish, even if it
wasn't winning. What surprises me is that there are still people
who think that "witnessing" like this is a put-on or a psychological crutch.

Jack would be the first to insist that witnessing for Christ
doesn't mean we've arrived at some near-perfect state. The
gospels remind us through the story of Peter's denial, the
doubts of Thomas, the treachery of Judas, and even the inner
torment of Jesus that the lot of man is to struggle. This is why I
envy those tough years that Jack and Jane shared with an

orange crate for a table and cinder blocks for chairs. It was not just adversity that shaped his character, but learning that hard work is necessary in tough times or easy ones. One has to work at being anything, including being a Christian.

The Sabbath, which is Sunday to Christians, is the symbol of rest—a day off from work. That even God rested seems a strange concept; surely this was the strongest pro-labor statement ever recorded. Sunday is our main day of work in the NFL, a day still considered so inviolable to many Christians that they would object no less to a game being held on this day than to a liquor store being open. Wouldn't it be ironic if a Christian message would filter into a few homes even from this unlikely source on a Sunday afternoon, when it failed to touch them from a church? Wouldn't it be appropriate if the work of the Lord would also have its place on a football field on the day of rest?

Jack Dolbin and I may never earn that Super Bowl victory ring, worth $3,000 or so. If we do, I know it will not eclipse the meaning of another ring he now wears so proudly, or the memory of that snow-driven Sunday in Hartford, when the thrill of a job well done was payment enough. And, for us both, the ultimate reward will be when Christ looks us in the eye and says, "Well done, good and faithful servant."

FIVE

TO BELIEVE IN REASON

TOM LANDRY

In the printing trade, duotones, or two-color halftones, are made by taking the same or similar screened negatives and positioning them slightly off one another. If the dots lie one on top the other, the second color will be assumed in the black. But when they are placed at a slight offset, the dots printed in red, blue, yellow, or whatever add a new dimension to the black plate. This image or technique comes to my mind whenever I think of that quintessential coach, Tom Landry.

I have already mentioned that when I was growing up in the Dallas organization I was unable to take the intense regimen that Coach Landry had developed for the Cowboys. I had to leave the room, on Monday morning screenings of the previous day's follies, because my stomach wouldn't take the criticism. Tom was a perfectionist—still is. But I'm happy to hear that he was going through a phase at that time as much as I was. He was growing; I was beginning to grow. The color in Tom Landry is now beginning to become visible to me, as the halftone dots of one side of his personality have begun to move away from the blackness that I once thought was all that was there.

Quintessential coach is what I call him; the game of pro football would not be complete without him—that image of the stone face, the computer-organized mind, the man in the business suit or very proper sports jacket and hat quietly pacing the sidelines. I know for a fact that he doesn't pursue that image for effect, as I imagine some coaches might. He is aware that the TV camera is always on him, or potentially on him. He never struts nor dodges before newspaper reporters. He is aware of their presence too, but he doesn't cater to it. More than all of this, he must be aware of the enigma he presents because of his religious orientation; he must know these inquiring journalists are after the *real* truth about Tom Landry, waiting for him to slip, to show him humanity. Little do they know that Coach Landry has a secret weapon now.

I can walk up to the Cowboys' imposing modern building on North Central Expressway in Dallas without any fear these days. I can go to the eleventh floor, greet the receptionist, and be ushered into the coach's office. Tom and I can sit down opposite each other and talk about our families and about the upcoming draft and about next year. For me it's a new dawn, because once I couldn't keep my breakfast down in his presence. For Landry it's a steady process of learning to be an adult human being, and the fact that he can easily admit he's changing is the thing that pulls me along with him into adulthood.

Tom Landry's secret weapon, the thing that allows me to look him straight in the eye, and that lets him rebound in victory or defeat, is his knowledge of the humanity of Christ. He is truly a fearless man and he knows why. "God does not give us fear," he likes to say these days, "but power and love and self-control. The thing that eats you up is fear and anxiety. Once you commit your life to Christ, it's in God's hands. He has a direction in which he wants to take you that isn't based on winning and losing." And the capper in this secret formula is this terse bit of psychology: *"The more you dwell on your own power, the more anxious you become."* Even if you don't place yourself in a higher power, even if you are a nonbeliever, this piece of advice can save you much heartache. If we're living in the age of anxiety, could the reason be that we have become addicted to our own power?

Other football players and journalists have also observed the subtle but powerful change that has gradually come over Landry. In 1974 Roger Staubach wrote, "Since I've known him he has gradually tried to get closer to the players, to bring his understanding of us more into the open. He still seems to me to be somewhat distant, with an infallible tone, but he is trying. The men have always respected him for his tremendous mind, but they respect him even more for trying to become closer to them." In this there is a paradox, for Landry has been a dedicated Christian, as opposed to a nominal Christian, for a long time. It was after the championship of the NFL in 1958, New York against Baltimore, a game Landry calls "the greatest game ever played," for it was the first and undoubtedly the most exciting *overtime* game in the books, that Landry accidentally had a brush with the meaning of Christianity. He had already reached one of the pinnacles in his life, playing on a championship team—the New York Giants fulfilled that ambition in 1956. On his return home to Dallas he ran into a friend who casually asked him if he wanted to join him in a Bible discussion at the Melrose Hotel. Landry says he thought to himself, "Man, you've got to be crazy. I've been going to church all my life. I know all the Christmas stories and everything else that goes with this thing, and I have a pretty good conscience. I know right from wrong." But—what the hell—he went along anyway. They handed him an open Bible and he started to read, "Therefore, do not be anxious about your life. . . do not be anxious about tomorrow . . . let the day's own trouble be sufficient for itself." He was thirty-three years old, and for the first time this book started making sense for him. The paradox is that some sixteen years later Staubach could write, "He still seems to me to be somewhat distant, with an infallible tone, but he is trying." The difficult truth is that no change occurs overnight, and any change that does seem to happen suddenly is superficial. To be "born again" doesn't mean to fall from heaven full grown.

On the eve of Super Bowl XIII, Skip Bayless of the *Dallas Morning News* tried to answer the question that has puzzled Cowboy fans and millions of TV viewers for years: Is Landry imperturbable, or is he chewing up knives and forks inside? How can he control his emotions, or doesn't he have any? The answer is that by 1979 Landry had grown just a little stronger, more closely in touch with his Lord. He told Bayless: "I don't want to come across as a pious type person. I suffer after losses, but fortunately I recover quickly. I have a source of power I wouldn't have without my relationship with Christ. As a Christian, I've gone through a maturing process. I've reached the point now where I feel no pressure in the Super Bowl."

Before you can digest that last statement, you have to look at what pressure and fear of failure have done to other coaches. Madden, Fairbanks, Prothro, Coryell, Shula, Malavasi have all experienced the gnawing pains of uncertainty, in the form of ulcers, high blood pressure, chain-smoking, heavy drinking, overeating, or insomnia. John Madden retired from one of the most successful teams in football, then found himself nervously pacing an empty house on Sundays in the fall. Landry knows all this, so he's quick to distinguish between the strength that flows into everything, including coaching, from his Christian commitment—and the idea of taking up Christianity in order to heal a bleeding ulcer. He's a better coach because of Christ, but Christ came first.

And there are many facets of the Landry personality, many sides of his character, that seem independent of his spiritual outlook. That stone-faced pose on the sidelines is not a product of a stoic demeanor—it's just the only way he can concentrate. "I very seldom look at the play," he confides; "I'm looking at the defense. So even when they put the camera on me, I haven't seen what the fans have seen. People get that picture of me. My image hasn't changed for eighteen years. I don't expect it to now." Landry says he picked this idea up partly from Ben Hogan: "He never cracked a smile—and he didn't hit many bad shots." The idea is to concentrate on the *doing* instead of the result. "Once you look at the scoreboard to see if you're doing it or not, you're dead. You're on your way to defeat." He saves his smiles for the postgame interview.

It's early in the fourth quarter of Super Bowl XIII, in January of 1979, with the three-point favorites, the men in black of the Pittsburgh Steelers, holding a four-point edge. They've driven deep into Cowboy territory, their first real drive of the second half, to take some of the momentum away from a pressing Dallas comeback. Then, on third down, Bradshaw unaccountably fails to get his team up to the line in time, and draws a five-yard penalty. Landry pulls on his chin, the only signal of relief from pressure. It's third and long, an obvious passing situation; the defensive signal is to blitz. The "dumb" Bradshaw rises to the situation with a beautiful call— a draw to Franco Harris. Franco pauses for a split second as the Dallas front wall surges by him, then he drives and spins straight up the middle—past the first down, past the safety, all the way for a touchdown.

Now down by 11, the Cowboys promptly fumble the ensuing kickoff. In the press box they're wondering if Landry can contain himself, or will he finally shatter the image and burn the fumbler's ears before 30 million TV viewers? He starts pacing, then pulls himself up short. On Bradshaw's first call he goes for a quick bomb. With the outside covered as if the Dallas secondary had been in the huddle, Lynn Swann cuts in behind the safety, Bradshaw reads him, and another six points are on the board. After the conversion it's now a laugher— 35–17.

Larry Cole, with the Cowboys since 1968, remembers what he told Skip Bayless in that pre-Super Bowl interview: "Before, when people were saying we couldn't win the big game, Landry would tell us before we played Cleveland or Green Bay that we just could not make a mistake. Now he says, 'We know we're going to make mistakes, but others will have to make up for them.' I wouldn't have played as long as I have if he wasn't the way he is." Cole is one of many in that stadium wondering how the second grave error sits with the coach. Someone will really have to make up for this one.

Staubach now begins to put on one of his patented performances. The Steeler defense is willing to give the short pass, but Roger starts playing the sidelines for big gainers. The first touchdown comes easy, and on the Pittsburgh bench Bradshaw yells at his teammates to stop celebrating. The public address system announces that Terry has set a Super Bowl passing record. He feels he's being hexed! With a few minutes to go Staubach is able to engineer another touchdown. Panic! Landry remembers the playoff game with the San Francisco Forty-Niners, when an on-side kick at just about this moment put the Cowboys back in the game. You will recall why I'll never forget that game, either. But this time the ball takes a different bounce, and Landry has to accept another defeat, as he did in Super Bowl XI, from Chuck Noll, 35–31.

What happened in January of 1979 was an omen for the rest of the year—the regular season of the following fall. From the very beginning Dallas had to struggle. The critical midseason game is always against archrival Washington, and this year the Redskins had a poor excuse for a welcome mat prepared for their friends. In the superheated atmosphere of the Washington stadium, the Cowboys committed mistake after mistake. Staubach took his lumps as the Redskins blitzed at will, especially on a passing down in their own territory. When the dust had settled, Dallas had to eke out another touchdown to make the losing cause appear honorable— 34–20. Landry began to feel some heat, too, back home. For the Dallas fans can be fickle—*not* to make the playoffs had become an unthinkable proposition. Most teams with a 5–4 record about this time are looking for miracles.

Landry tightened the defense, began to get the bounces going his way. Washington seemed a clear winner of the division, so the Cowboys pointed to a wild-card berth. Then, the weekend before the final clash with the Redskins, Dallas got a break. The Redskins lost, Dallas won. The season would now come down to their rematch. The winner would take the division, the loser would presumably be the wild card. But this

time the game would be in Dallas, or, more exactly, Irving—the
site of Texas Stadium.

Despite all the X's and O's, the flex defense, the stern
concentration of Tom Landry, and a sympathetic crowd, the
Cowboys seemed destined to repeat their earlier debacle. As
the final quarter ticked away, the score was almost identical to
the final count of the previous meeting—34–21 in favor of the
Redskins. Washington seemed to be playing with reckless
abandon, for the playoffs were in their hands in any case, so it
seemed. There was the insane possibility that the Chicago
Bears would run up a huge score in their last game, and thus
edge Washington in the event they had equal won-lost records.
So the stage was set for another comeback try by a Staubach
who had apparently gone to the well once too often.

The insane, thank goodness, sometimes happens. Washington was sitting on the ball, sitting on its lead, when, with but
a few minutes remaining, came the fumble. The Cowboys
recovered, and Staubach hit immediately for the touchdown.
Landry says half a dozen or so games passed through his mind,
all involving Roger and his two-minute offense. He lined up his
plays, as he customarily does, three in advance—waiting,
hoping for Washington to have to punt. When their third-down
conversion failed, Landry slapped his hands together. "At
least now we have a shot at it. One shot, for the championship,
for the playoffs."

Staubach was now the essence of concentration, the Redskins were bewildered. The plays came in one after another
and down he drove to the Washington eight, first and goal.
There's something about being ahead by a mere six points, as
Washington was, 34–28, with time running out and the other
team knocking at your door. If they score, there's no time to
shoot even for a field goal. In the NFL, how many teams would
choose to be ahead in this situation? But if you don't score,
your suffering is almost worse—because you *should* have.

There were 42 seconds on the clock as Staubach came to
the line of scrimmage. Landry had sent in a hook pattern to
Billy Joe DuPree in the left flat. But in the huddle Staubach
entered a disclaimer. There's a blitz coming, he thought—like
the wild charges that had leveled him in the first game between

these two games. Just in case, he told wide receiver Tony Hill on the other flank, run a quick nine. The "quick nine" is a nod and a spurt dead ahead—sheer speed to get the extra step over short distances. If the blitz appears, all the quarterback has to do is float it up there where his receiver is supposed to be. It's not quite a blind play, but almost—sort of like a suicide squeeze in baseball: if it works at all, it's all over. As he made a long count, Staubach spotted two defenders shading toward DuPree. His mind was made up—Hill would be one-on-one, and Landry would do the same thing in his shoes. Lemar Parrish, the cornerback on Hill's side, was playing him tight, so that when Staubach took a step back Hill was already nudging past Parrish. The ball headed to the corner of the end zone, where Hill arrived at the proper moment to smother it to his chest. A stunned Redskin defensive unit wandered off the field, unbelieving. The game was over. Dallas had won the championship, 35–34. Worse, Washington was no longer in the playoffs, for on the scoreboard, as if by mistake, an outrageously lopsided score in the Chicago game was posted. The Bears would be the wild card!

Staubach had created another impossible finish. The thirty-seven-year-old quarterback had combined with the thirty-four-year-old Preston Pearson for two long-gainers in that last drive, and had made the thinking man's call on the final play of the game. This was not in Landry's game plan. But with the new Landry these calls would have been acceptable even if they had failed.

In the mid-sixties, the Cowboys lost two NFL championship games in successive years to the Green Bay Packers—both in the last seconds. In the first of these games, Dallas had first and goal on the Packers' two-yard line, and failed to score. When Landry is asked whether he called those four crucial plays, he replies with the following story of a friend who coached a high school team in New Jersey some years ago.

It seems that everything had come down to the last game of the season; whoever won took the championship. The coach was especially nervous as the last quarter approached and his team had fallen behind by four points. A field goal wouldn't do, and their offense was sputtering. It didn't help matters that a little third-string quarterback kept jumping up and down in front of the coach—like a puppy dog brushing against his feet—hoping to get in the game. The opposing team was eating up the clock with every possession. At last, with a minute to go, they made a first down and the game was as good as over. Then, with no time-outs remaining, the opponents fumbled on first down and lost the ball. In his excitement the coach pushed the third-string quarterback onto the field and shouted, "Run seven to the right and six to the left!"

The little guy barely got his helmet on, but he barked out the calls without a huddle and sent the team down to the one-yard line on the two plays. The lock was ticking down to the fifteen second mark—time for one more play. The little quarterback looked to the sidelines for another play, but the coach could only yell "Get into that huddle and run something!" Miraculously, the team broke the huddle and got the play off before the clock had gone down to zero. But what was going on? The coach watched in horror as a double reverse unfolded on the field. He closed his eyes, and then the roar of the crowd made him look up: the runner went into the end zone untouched! The coach dared not mention that unbelievable call until the players stopped celebrating, showered, and got on the bus back to their own school. Then he sidled up to the little fellow. "Tell me, Billy," he said with fatherly restraint, "why did you pick that double reverse with only a yard to go? In fact, it looked like a foot to go. You could have sneaked it over, or wedged the fullback right, or even rolled out."

"Well, coach, I was confused. You told me to run a seven, and then a six, and when you didn't give me a third play I just added them together and came up with fourteen. And that's our double reverse."

The coach thought that over, then smiled a devil-may-care smile. "Billy, that's some reasoning. But six and seven are thirteen, not fourteen."

"Hey, you're sure right, coach. But if I were as smart as you, we wouldn't have won that game, would we?"

Landry says, "So maybe you can see why I don't call any

plays when we're down on the goal line. I turn it all over to my quarterback. I figure he's got to be smarter than I am when he's down there."

Tom has been in charge of the Cowboys now for more than twenty years. Before that, he was an All-Pro defensive back for the New York Giants, an outstanding halfback at the University of Texas, and an all-district running back in his hometown high school in Mission, Texas. It was in this little world, a community of but 6,000, that Tom grew up in the Depression and dreamed of making something big out of his life. It was a restlessness, he explains, that's different from the urge to go to the big city or explore the world. It was the beginning of a search for some kind of meaning in this little speck of life in the vast, seemingly ageless universe.

At first he thought that meaning might be found in football, in the thrill of the game and the headiness of success— even if it was only Mission, Texas. A championship, perhaps, or being picked for an all-star team. He got both; in his senior year his team was scored on only once. He was elated for a few months, but the thrill wore off. Now he began to think that the real thing was college football, and the best, of course, was the game played at the University of Texas. He set his sights on making the Texas team, and if he made it to a bowl game life would be complete. Tom was developing into a pretty quick running back—he even looked the part, with a handsome western face, broad shoulders, and a ramrod-straight physique. In his junior and senior years he helped his team make it to both the Sugar Bowl and the Orange Bowl. He was on top of the world! He was co-captain, and they beat Alabama and Georgia.

Landry's life had become a series of plateaus, which he thought must lead to satisfaction in life. Like a management consultant mapping out goals for a corporation, he plotted his objectives in the professional game. If he couldn't make it as a running back, he'd use his size and speed as a defensive back. He'd be a star in a major city. He'd make the All-Pro team. He'd play for the National Football League championship. And so he did.

On top of everything, he had the woman of his dreams as

his wife, and was raising a family with Alicia in Dallas. Soon there was a Tom, Jr., then Kitty and Lisa. Winning was part of his life: games, honors, success, respectability, love. He now shifted to coaching, with the Giants, and began to apply the industrial engineering background he had from college days to the task of devising defensive systems. It was another plateau, for he was now using his mind, he was a part of a scientific endeavor and not a mere athlete. His complex alignments and shifts of defensive backs were something new in pro football, and more than just fans were beginning to take note of this man with the stone face.

It was at this critical juncture, at thirty-three years of age, at the top of his profession, that the meeting with a Bible group at a hotel in Dallas changed his life. Nothing was more unlikely to challenge the emptiness in Landry's inner life than sitting around a table discussing a passage from the New Testament. "My scientific approach to everything in life made it hard for me to accept many things in Scripture," he says. "I felt nothing could change my direction. When I used to drive from town to town as an insurance salesman in the off-season, I'd play those motivational tapes put out by supersalesmen. It was all rah-rah stuff. Some of them would quote the Bible, but as a way to buck up your courage and give you self-confidence. After a few days you couldn't remember half of what was said, and in a month you were right back where you started." He had everything to make a man happy; maybe this was all there is to life, he reasoned—just setting goals and achieving them. But now he began to do something Tom Landry never really thought much about before. He began to *listen.*

The great Yankee pitcher Ron Guidry recently recounted how his life took a turn because he learned, one day, to listen. In the early part of the 1976 season he was spending more than his share of playing time in the bullpen. He had a nice rising fastball, a wife, and a child, which is not too bad for a twenty-five-year-old. But his future in the game looked rocky. Two more seasoned pitchers, Sparky Lyle and Dick Tidrow, advised him to work on a slider and his pitching speeds. He knew that Lyle was the master of the slider and that Tidrow was an expert at keeping the batter guessing, but he was stubborn.

One fateful day, facing Boston's Carl Yastrzemski with a man on base, he decided to wave off all the signals and blaze three fastballs past the "old man." Yaz took two of them and put the third one in the upper deck. After that Ron found himself spending even more time in the bullpen, and then was sent down to Syracuse. He was on his way back to his home in Louisiana when his wife Bonnie talked him into sticking it out in the minors. "Bonnie and I decided to pray about changing my stubborn attitude, about doing things my own way." He worked on Lyle's and Tidrow's advice at Syracuse, and made it back to the Yankees the following year. There he went from a 16–7 record in 1977 to an unbelievable 25–3 in 1978. "There are many things in life I still don't know," he sums up, "but one thing I do know: When a more experienced person offers advice, *listen!*"

Landry began to listen, not so much to preachers or businessmen-friends, but to this person in the Gospels. After all, he hadn't even listened to his father, a Sunday-school superintendent for thirty-seven years, when he told him that a football game is a small fragment of one's total life. But now Christ's words challenged him. Who was this man? Was he a real historical figure, or a pleasant myth? Over and over Landry had heard the skeptics argue that God is something man would invent to satisfy his cravings for something larger than himself—what did it matter if God existed or not? Now the figure of Christ had to be dealt with, for, says Landry, "If I accepted Him, then I accepted what He said; and if I accepted what he said, then there was something unsatisfying in the way I was living my life."

It was this burr that Christ was bringing into his life that almost turned him away from studying the Bible further. It was uncomfortable. But he wanted to hear Christ out. He began to call him The Challenger. For, in the Gospel of Matthew, it is an angry, demanding Jesus that confronts the reader, the listener. "Every kingdom divided against itself is brought to desolation, and every city or house divided against itself will not stand." Landry particularly began thinking about a house built on rock: ". . . and the rain fell, and the floods came, and the winds blew and beat on that house, but it did not fall. . . ."

What kind of foundation, he wondered, was he really building for his family? What was he building for himself?

Landry found himself going back to those Bible discussions, simply to help answer the nagging question, "How can we be sure Jesus is who He says he is?" He admits now that the answers he got at first were unsatisfying. He took to doing his own research. And he applied the measurements he had learned as a football coach: "You train players to accomplish certain objectives—a place kicker to put three points on the board on most tries within the fifty-yard line, a passer to hit his targets ninety percent of the time, and so forth. During each game we keep a chart on the players' efficiency in carrying out their assignments. Over the years I've found that high scores on the charts correlate well with a high winning percentage." It may sound calculating and cold, but charts present an objective measurement when the heat of battle obscures the observer's judgment. Landry undertook to do nothing less than chart Jesus!

"I couldn't help but think of Him except in terms of what He did—what He accomplished in His life. His record, the impact of His life on millions of people through the centuries, is, to say the least, impressive. To a rational mind, it's a compelling argument. But I saw something else, too." Landry was won over by the fact that Christ offered another plateau that was so far above anything he had set his sights on that it had to be explored. It was the mountaintop, nothing less. The mind of Jesus was tough, unswerving, relentless. He parried the subtle objections of the existing hierarchy of his native religion with finesse and firmness. "Render therefore to Caesar the things that are Caesar's and to God the things that are God's." Or, "What man among you who has one sheep, if it falls into a pit on the Sabbath, will not lay hold of it and lift it out? Of how much more value is a man than a sheep? Therefore it is lawful to do good on the Sabbath." Or, "O brood of vipers! How can you, being evil, speak good things? For out of the abundance of the heart the mouth speaks."

Landry's intellectual pursuit of the historical Jesus didn't end in a flash of recognition, a conversion (not the three-point kind!), or a careful calculation of the odds on there being a hell or a heaven. At some point in the spring of 1959, before he took over the head coaching job at the new Dallas Cowboys, he recalls putting his arguments aside. "All my intellectual questions no longer seemed important, and I had a curiously joyous feeling inside." He had received that gift of faith that theologians talk about. Paul Tillich writes, "Faith is not a theoretical affirmation of something uncertain, it is the . . . acceptance of something transcending ordinary experience." It is not a belief in something unbelievable; "faith is not an opinion but a state." That curiously joyous feeling was to grow as a seed within him. And he wanted to share it.

Jim Zorn says that one day he'd like to tell Tom Landry what an effect it had on him when, in his tryout for the Cowboys in 1975, Tom began a squad meeting with a reference to his own Christian attitude toward competition. With Paul, he was ready to fight the good fight, to run the good race. Jim recalls that Landry's reference to the Bible was factual and not preachy, but gave him a lift he has never forgotten.

Landry has given the Cowboys every opportunity to deepen their spiritual lives—through prayer meetings, nondenominational services before games, and the like—but he doesn't foist his beliefs off on anyone. Are there players who toady up to the Coach by trying to play on his religious commitment? "You mean, are there con artists in this game?" he laughs. "It's always difficult to be objective in interpersonal relations. I try to be as honest as I can." I know several players who are quite silent about their religious beliefs, even though they coincide with those of Coach Landry. There is a sort of silent communication between them, and that's the way they want it to remain.

Landry is a much sought-after speaker, and is known to interject his "witness" to Christ in every talk. Yet it's done so honestly and matter-of-factly that most of his listeners find it as natural as talking about the flex defense. He has set priorities all his life, and now they come down to these three: God, family, football. Under "family," I think, he would include "people," because long ago he started to make that shift in character that changed him from a one-dimensional, all-scientific autocrat into a caring good neighbor. So he is often asked, "You must spend sixteen hours a day on football. How can you wedge God and family in?" He answers, "God and family permeate everything I do. There are no partitions in life." Bringing God into his daily life, he says, changed the way he conducted his coaching duties. "I began to think a little less about football and a little more about the people involved in it."

Not unexpectedly, a man of the intensity, ambitions, and qualities of Tom Landry attracts the media. Only a person in the public limelight—a governor, a senator, the President—inspires cartoonists and satirists. Much of the lampooning is cruel—as in the stick-figure of a coach in the movie, *North Dallas Forty*. Landry takes it all in good humor, for he respects the intelligence and outlook of his former players. He's been there himself. Peter Gent says, "I do know this. During the first couple of years after I left football, there was no justification for living. It was a nightmare. Life just had no meaning compared to catching a football. . . . Some days, the only reason I got to work was because Jody dressed me and combed my hair." If football was his god, Coach Landry was, in an ironic sense, its high priest. Gent continues:

> *Look, Landry's a man of history. He's a brilliant football tactician. I've been with him, and I've experienced things with him. Like everyone else connected with the Cowboys, I have an emotional relationship with the man. I've seen him cry in locker rooms, get mad. And yet there's a whole part of him that's not there.*

Landry would take this comment—especially in these, his middle years—with an emotion akin to gratitude. He believes in the adversary system, even when it comes to character development. True, he will send in the plays even to men as shrewd as Eddie LeBaron or Don Meredith or Roger Staubach. "It's tough for a quarterback to size up the defense, see the changing pattern of the game, call the plays, and remember all the keys. Most people don't realize how intellectually tough a game this is." But when the ball gets inside the five-yard line, the heat of the battle changes the nature of the contest. It's then that sheer competitive spirit dictates the plays. And that's when Landry remembers the third-string quarterback who called the double reverse on the goal line.

The 1979 season ended for Dallas in 1979: there would be no trip to the Super Bowl for the Cowboys this year. There was something almost biblical about the story of the playoffs, something about how he who humbles himself will be exalted, about how the last shall be first. Of all things, there was Tampa Bay earning a match-up with Pittsburgh for the championship of the AFC. And Dallas would have the Los Angeles Rams for dinner.

The Rams had been doormats for the Cowboys in play-offs over the years, and this time they would have to make the journey to Texas Stadium to take their lumps. A typically confident Dallas crowd cheered the hometown team through four predictable quarters. This was duck soup compared to that end-of-the-season thriller with Washington. The Landry machine ground away, always keeping a little edge. Now, with the last few minutes ticking off, the fans were looking forward to another Super Bowl clash with Pittsburgh. Then the stadium went strangely silent. As a national TV audience looked on unbelievingly, the Rams got the ball back on a Dallas turnover and suddenly struck with a slant-in pass over the middle by their unheralded number two quarterback, Vince Ferragamo. There was no shotgun-formation comeback by Staubach. A team with a struggling 9–7 record in league play had beaten the mighty Cowboys, had ended a jinx, had outfoxed the coach with the computer mind.

Tom Landry waited patiently in the dressing room for more than an hour, answering embarrassing questions about crucial calls, critical bounces of the ball. He didn't say, "So much of coaching is out of your control," as he did when asked to comment a year before about Tommy Prothro's record with San Diego. He didn't dispute some questionable decisions by the referees. "When you need the breaks going all your way to win a close game, you're not a deserving winner." Yes, he still feels intensely that he wants to be the finest coach in the game, that the Cowboys should be the most successful team on the planet. But if he had to walk out of that interview to be fired from the team he loves he would see it as part of a larger plan. Even football, and even meaningless losses in football, have their reasons.

One of the reasons Landry sees is football's potential to reach young people with a spiritual message. This is the guiding principle of an organization dear to Tom's heart—as it is to mine and to the hearts of dozens of my colleagues in athletics.

Back in 1949, when professional sports was just emerging from the restrictions of the Second World War and when football was definitely a poor relation to big league baseball, a basketball coach, an evangelistic Christian in the Midwest got a brazen idea. He wondered why Jesus Christ couldn't be sold by endorsements from popular professional athletes. Now, it takes some courage to proclaim a "sissy" thing like religion if you're a he-man, so no one was worried that athletes would claim they loved Jesus if they didn't mean it. But—how to find athletes to speak out? How to organize them?

The coach wangled an appointment with Branch Rickey, who was then with the Pittsburgh Pirates and was known to have Christian beliefs. Rickey didn't quite understand what this "fanatic" had in mind, but he agreed to spend five minutes with him. The interview lasted all afternoon. And thus was born the Fellowship of Christian Athletes.

Perhaps this organization will never come to more than a meeting ground for like-minded individuals, a beachhead of Christian thinking in the ocean of materialistic American sports. I think it's a powerful force at many levels, but no matter. If all it ever did was to crystallize Branch Rickey's thinking, it performed yeoman service. For Mr. Rickey undoubtedly was influenced by this sign of the changing role of the athlete when, with the Dodgers a few years later, he opened the doors of professional sports to the black athlete in the person of Jackie Robinson. In 1956 our organization had its first regular camp, when that great quarterback, Otto Graham, welcomed his fellow athletes to a one-week meeting at Estes Park, Utah. Ever since then, the first week or so of June has been set aside for these conclaves. There we learn from each other, amateurs and pros alike, both to support our own commitment and to share it with college kids. Since 1966 the FCA has also sponsored a "huddle" program to reach high school athletes, and more recently an effort to share our concerns with women at the high school and college level has been underway.

As one of the senior members of the fellowship, Landry has been a persuasive leader in this cause. "Kids today are far more advanced in many ways than we were," he explains. "If you have teenage kids, you may know why. They form their character at an earlier age. If you don't get 'em before they are too far along in high school, they'll be set on a course from which there's no turning back." Landry and his generation grew up in hard times—several years of a depression followed by a war that challenged the very idea of goodness in mankind. Even into the 1950's there was always a spectre of hard times ahead, and top professional athletes had yet to hear of agents and multimillion dollar contracts. As Landry moved into coaching, he saw young men come up from college without a scratch of adversity showing. They had scholarships, cars, guarantees of jobs, and the vast potential of television to make them household words if they hit the top. I know, because I was one of them. The shock waves of the affluent society had spread into high school athletics, too. "I began to worry about how these emotionally immature people would handle the accolades of fans, the big cars, drugs, alcohol, sex," says Landry. "To no one's surprise, a good many of them didn't." Vince Lombardi's famous quote, about winning not being the main thing, but the only thing, was a matter of faith for this generation. It doesn't matter that Lombardi, as Landry says, meant it in a very qualified way. It became a battle cry in the rush for instant success.

Landry's theory about nonbelievers is that they are at a stage of development through which they must inevitably pass before becoming believers. Nowadays, however, that stage is liable to become set in concrete, he feels, because the elements of character building that his generation relied on are missing from our society. "I think I can understand the nonbeliever's attitude," he says. "I've been there. It must be

harder for him to understand mine. In my experience, the only
way to make a real change in one's life, to make a gut change in
character, is through Jesus Christ."

Landry easily acknowledges that he learned something
about freedom from the new generation, too. It's difficult to
see a need for Christ when you're riding high, he points out.
It's easier to rely on people, not some higher power. And that
fact makes one more open, more human. Landry concedes that
his mental outlook foreclosed on his early development as a
caring person. His big regret is that it took him thirty-three
years to open up to the message of Christ. As Skip Bayless
writes, "Landry the perfectionist, Landry the dictator, wasn't
easy to live with, to work for. He couldn't begin to understand
the flakes, the mavericks, those individually oriented, those
who gave eighty percent. Now he gives them a chance." Now
he can look back and say, "The way I looked at people began
to change. I started looking outside myself and enjoying
people for the first time."

We live in a surprisingly unscientific world. Ask anyone
his astrological sign, and he'll tell you. Pick up a copy of any of
the national newspapers sold in supermarkets, and you'll see
what most of us human beings are interested in: magic, predic-
tions of the future, biorhythms, miracle cures. And we tend to
confuse religion with magic, with voices from the grave, with
wishful thinking about an afterlife. People like Tom Landry
have shown the courage to use their heads instead of blindly
showing up at church on Sunday mornings. "Christians have a
great advantage," he says with a smile. "Remember, it's how
you *think* in this world that makes you successful. If you have a
positive attitude, good things will happen. Maybe if positive
thinking has become a million-dollar industry, it's something
we should pay attention to. But really, those people are just
teaching what God gives us in the Bible." Then he chuckles.
"That sounds a little materialistic, doesn't it?"

In a society that makes little attempt to change character
in its young people—recklessly permissive on the one hand
and cruelly unscientific on the other, such as in its prisons—
football may have a role to play that its inventors and present
practitioners scarcely intended. Football teaches character,

Landry maintains; any form of adversity, competition, stress does. We have laughed that proposition off as an old-fashioned notion concocted by hard-bitten coaches. Perhaps football has this higher purpose only by showing how interdependent all men and women are on this earth, this speck of time in which we are granted to discover something about the meaning of life. For if football brought us nothing else, it produced a Tom Landry. No less a thinker than Albert Einstein proposed the dilemma that neatly sums up, in nonreligious terms, the search that Landry has undergone:

> *Strange is our situation here upon earth. Each of us comes for a short visit, not knowing why, yet sometimes seeming to divine a purpose. From the standpoint of daily life, however, there is one thing we do know: that man is here for the sake of other men . . . for the countless unknown souls with whose fate we are connected by a bond of sympathy. Many times a day I realize how much my own outer and inner life is built upon the labors of my fellow men, both living and dead, and how earnestly I must exert myself in order to give in return as much as I have received and am still receiving.*

SIX

TO BELIEVE IN PEOPLE

RED MILLER

When we arrived in Pittsburgh in late October of 1979 to meet the Steelers in a Monday-night football showdown, we knew we would be tangling with a wounded bear. The previous week they had fumbled nine times to be mauled by the Cincinnati Bengals, 34–10. Chuck Noll, we heard, had set up a mini-camp in midweek to bring his charges up to speed. The papers said that Lynn Swann would be back, injured or not.

He came back quickly, taking a Terry Bradshaw bomb in the first quarter for a difficult touchdown. Our All-Pro cornerback Louis Wright went up with him in the end zone, but when they came down Swann had the ball. That's the kind of a score Red Miller could forgive. Characteristically, he began talking it up with the defense along the sidelines: "C'mon now, pull together!" This was no time to get rattled, with TV cameras everywhere and a Pittsburgh crowd eager for blood.

It was hard to believe anybody could beat this team by twenty-four points: they came back down the field as the second period opened, slanting, bucking, spinning to our twenty-one. Then they came up to the line in an unexpected formation. John Stallworth lined up with Swann on the right, and a reserve wide receiver we hadn't seen much of, Jim Smith, drifted out to the left. Miller considers coaching to be a game of wits, a sort of floating chessboard on which the offensive coaching staff tries to outthink the opponent's defensive alignment. There are always human errors, to be sure; the chess pieces don't always move the way they are supposed to. But this time Miller felt something coming at him from that mini-camp of Chuck Noll's. Bradshaw stepped back into the pocket, getting that extra second of protection that allows the patterns to run their course. Sure enough, Stallworth and Swann drew our cornerbacks along with them, leaving Smith one on one with our deep safety. When a quarterback has the full sight of the field and doesn't have to move to meet the rush, there's no way to defend against a good pass. Smith caught it at the two, and on the next play Franco Harris was in for the second touchdown. The Broncos, who always prided themselves on being tough inside the twenty, were being *outthought.*

Later in the same quarter, after another Steeler score, they came down again near our twenty and lined up the same way. It was almost an instant replay: Smith hooked in for a completion at the one, and Sidney Thornton dove over to make it 28–0. The three-man wide receiver attack had hit us before we could correct against it. When we finally staggered off the field it was 42–7, the most points we had given up in five seasons and sixty-three games. Miller was devastated: "It's the most humiliating defeat in the thirty years I've been associated with football. We were outplayed, outcoached, and embarrassed in front of a lot of people." On the other side of the field, Noll was telling reporters, "That's the Steeler team I know. We had everybody functioning in every department. It was as simple as that." For us, it was a little deeper than that.

Our defense wasn't performing the miracles it had for the past
three years. And it wasn't because the chess game was being
won by the offense. We used to flood the defensive backfield
with eight fast men, and defy the Terry Bradshaws of the world
to find a man open. As my teammate, Bob Swenson, puts it,
"It used to be the quarterback would throw the ball and somebody he didn't see would pick it off. We don't have as many
interceptions now, because teams are getting used to seeing
that many guys back there. Point totals are up all over the
league, and we're giving them up like everybody else."

Red Miller came to the Broncos in 1977, and immediately made such an impact—winning the AFC for the first time
in Denver and going to the Super Bowl—that the Orange
Crush became identified with his tenure. Actually, the great
defensive innovations of the Broncos had an earlier origin. In
1972 the Miami Dolphins came up with a switch on the
standard defensive alignment of four men on the line. One of
the four, Bob Matheson, number 53, had the skills to play the
line as well as a linebacker slot: he was both big and fast.
Duplicity then entered his mind: why not keep the offense
guessing by lining up with the other three, then dropping back
or charging as the situation dictated? If you've ever played
touch football, you've seen the same thing on a looser scale.
But even pro football has become so structured that a touch-
football idea becomes an "innovation" when grown men try
something different. Because of Matheson's number, they
dubbed it the "53 defense," but it was essentially a variable
3–4 defense: three men at the line most of the time, and four
linebackers most of the time, instead of vice versa. Because
the Dolphins went on to win Super Bowl VII that year—mainly
due to their tremendous ground game—the defense gained
some adherents.

But a genuine three-man defensive line was uncommon
until 1975, when the Broncos struck upon it almost by necessity. You have to remember that this was a talented team—
brought up from doormat status by the organizational abilities
of Fred Gerhke and by the methodical John Ralston—which
still had not achieved the self-confidence to hope for a championship. In the middle of that season, Denver was being

rolled over by the traditionally powerful Bengals. In the late stages of that game, suffering from injuries in their defensive backfield, the Broncos tried to stem the tide by pulling a man off the line to give more pass coverage on the wings. They were successful enough to hold the score to a 17–16 squeaker. So they experimented with it in four more games that year, convincing even the opposing coaches that they had a workable idea. The following year they worked it out more methodically, and the Orange Crush, by a variety of names, became a recognizable strategic defense. Their record of 9–5 in 1976 would have won a division or league championship in many another year. The Oakland Raiders, never a team to miss a bet, plugged in their own version of the 3–4 and went to the Super Bowl that year.

As a relatively young organization, however, the Broncos could experiment with more than defenses. A group of the players, not satisfied with the success of the team, petitioned the owners to find a more aggressive coach. As bad as it sounds, Bob Swenson says, this wasn't a revolt against bad handling by the head coach: "Ralston did a lot for the Broncos. But at one point the players realized we had a lot of talent and weren't winning as much as we should. We voted for a change." Thus it was that a search went out after the 1976 season for a new coach, and that Red Miller returned to Denver. It was highly significant that a coach like Red would find his way to the top by the accident of a popular vote.

Robert Miller is the son of a coal miner from a small town, Macomb, in southern Illinois. He was just old enough as a schoolboy to experience the effects of the Great Depression. Football became for him a way, perhaps the only way, to get a higher education. At Western Illinois he played the game sixty minutes, offense and defense, as a guard and linebacker. Over his three varsity years he was elected the team's most valuable player—quite a feat for a lineman when you think about who usually gets the headlines. He moved quite naturally into high school and college coaching, for he had an understanding of motivation that had been an essential part of his own survival as a small-town, small-college athlete. He began to realize that the single most important thing to people is—other people.

As he entered his career in professional football coaching, Red gravitated toward offense. Even in football, he reasoned, it's the best defense, since a more aggressive team always leaves the opposition with an inferior field position. The defensive platoon that gets only three plays and a punt from its offense, time after time, is more easily worn down. He signed on with Lou Saban's staff at the Boston Patriots in 1960 and moved to Buffalo with Saban in 1962. Then he came out to Denver as offensive line coach for three years. But coaching is an uncertain occupation and many a man becomes a nomad as the winds of popularity shift. Red moved on to St. Louis and Baltimore, again as offensive line coach, until tapped by Chuck Fairbanks to take over the offense of the New England Patriots in 1973. It was there that he built up his reputation for moving the ball; in his fourth year with the Patriots the team was second in the NFL in points scored and fifth in all NFL history in rushing.

What is it that makes an offense gel? Is it a fortunate combination of personnel? After all, he did have Steve Grogan, the man who set an NFL record for touchdowns run in by a quarterback—twelve. Or is it a lucky schedule, the breaks, the off days of the opponents? How many times would Cincinnati expect to run up thirty-four points over Pittsburgh? All these things can account for some offensive success, but not over a twenty-year period. Miller developed five All-Pro offensive linemen at St. Louis and three at New England. It's his opinion that it's the team effort that pays off, not the success of any one superstar.

Red and I came to Denver in 1977 relatively unknown to each other. I knew him briefly when I was with the Giants, but I was unaware of his philosophy. It quickly became apparent that he was unlike any coach I had met before. He talked about the "coming together of personalities," about "caring for common goals and forgetting personal egos." Yes, he also said that every pass, every block, every rush would be charted and recharted. But in the end he based his decisions—who would play and who wouldn't—upon personal qualities. His criterion for selecting a quarterback was primarily who could lead the team under stress. And his manner of encouraging those qualities was—and is—the difference between a coach who talks a good game and one who performs.

Miller is able to know his players without catering to them. He's able to understand their personal problems without becoming a den mother. He's well balanced enough to earn their trust and loyalty without losing the right to criticize and reprove them. After our great comeback victory over Seattle in 1979, I felt I had earned a shot at starting a game instead of waiting until someone else had trouble. Yet even in the flush of a great victory, Red told reporters he would reserve judgment about who would start the following Sunday. "We'll probably go with Weese and have Craig Morton ready," he said. "A lack of good field position hurt Norris in the first half when he was trying to move the team. He never got the ball in better position than the twenty-one." I had to agree, in spite of my eagerness to play. It was a typical Miller *team* decision.

In that game, incidentally, every one of us knew something that never showed up in the newspapers until well after the season was over. When I went in our telephone system broke down. Our scouts upstairs were unable to call in plays or information about Seattle's defensive alignment. Red was therefore in the dark, and had to let me call the plays as I saw them. Because of some great defensive breaks, we were able to score twenty-one points in the next two or three minutes. Yet I also felt proud of my reading of the defense—I had been watching it from the bench. It wasn't a big thing, but it might have revived that old argument about whether the coach or the quarterback is in a better position to make the offensive decisions. As a team, we let it pass. But as the 1980 season rolled around, Red decided to get some backup for his play calling. When the Broncos fell short of the playoffs that year, he was fired by the new management—ironically, in search of more offense!

A quarterback's ego takes a lot of beating on the subject of comparisons with other QBs. This is why Terry Bradshaw says he prefers not to read the papers in the middle of the season. If you have a great game, who can resist? It's like reliving the game. Even fans who attend a game, watch the reruns on the late news, listen to summaries on the radio, still want to read a complete account of the whole thing the next day in the newspaper—especially if their team wins. Our quarterback coach was once quoted in midweek about me: "He's throwing better than the year we went to the Super Bowl. We've always said he could if he got the time, and he is. I've seen a lot of great quarterbacks, and I'll tell you something. Right now, Morton is throwing with any of them." That's the great Babe Parilli talking, and who wouldn't want to hear that? In the same column, Red Miller was asked about a statement by John Madden that only five quarterbacks in the NFL were capable of consistently leading his team on scoring drives in every game (and Morton wasn't among them). Red graciously defended me: "I rate a man on his ability to get his team into the end zone, but, my God, not on that alone. Guys who can do it without a great supporting cast would certainly have to be included." And he mentioned that I was able to get the job done many times under trying circumstances. So far, so good. These are the subjects that columnists love to write about in midweek, when the previous Sunday's game has already been forgotten. But when things aren't going so well—such as when we could barely get a touchdown in the last few games of the 1979 season—it's not so easy to "relive" the game in the newspapers. That's when I appreciate Red's honesty the most. Just as there's no artificial pep talk in his praise, there's no backbiting in his criticisms. He knows that people respond to this. He gives people credit for being as adult as he is. *He puts himself in their place.*

Red is well aware that several of his players are openly Christian, and he has seen Christian influences throughout his coaching career. Chuck Fairbanks, for example, was to the University of Colorado and to the Patriots what Tom Landry was and is to the Cowboys. And Red worked closely with Chuck. Yet the Denver coach prefers not to witness his own faith openly. "Whatever I could say about my beliefs," he says, "could never be as convincing as what I *do*." It's one of the paradoxes of the human condition that two people can be as different as Landry and Miller, and still be excellent examples of Christlike behavior. Miller follows the example laid down by

Christ in His story of the hypocritical Pharisee who prays in public compared to the widow who makes her contribution without fanfare. When you fast, He says, don't go around with a long face to show everybody what you're doing. When you pray, do it in the privacy of your room. None of this contradicts the other Christian admonition to let your light shine openly for others to see. In his own way, Coach Miller knows the Christian message. As Jack Dolbin puts it, "He has a private walk with the Lord."

"I can remember back to the time I was in the sixth, seventh, and eighth grades—I always wanted to be a coach. I guess I'm one of the lucky people in life, because I got just what I wanted." Even as Red says this, he sweeps away any doubt that life is a lottery; his quiet determination shows where he stands. "I've always wanted to do more than the ordinary," he admits; "and the only way to do that is to set a goal, accomplish it, and set another one." He feels slightly uncomfortable with prayer meetings or public Bible readings, but he knows these things have been quite effective with people unlike himself. He tolerates what works for people. Since the things that have influenced his life have been the personal example of others, this is what he tries to offer by his own life. I know this: he suffers with us on that field!

In one of the lesser known letters of Paul, to the Hebrews, there is a striking appeal to us to accept people, to believe in them *on faith*. I think Red practices this is an outstanding way, on and off the field. He's not terribly interested in *socializing* with other coaches and players, or with reporters or charity organizers. But he is completely trusting of people in the *jobs* they expect to do. He practices what Paul recommends:

> *Do not forget to entertain strangers, for by this some have unwittingly entertained angels.*

The subject of motivation is fast becoming a hot topic in professional sports. Coaches in track and field now routinely make the claim that performance is 50 percent talent and training, and 50 percent motivation. Can that be? Wouldn't a coach rather have an unmotivated superstar rather than a highly motivated free agent? Perhaps. But motivation nowadays means a lot more than a half-time pep talk.

I always think of motivation in reference to Red Miller because of how I reacted to other coaches. Under Tom Landry—the "old" Landry—I thought I performed fairly well, even though I was motivated more by the fear of failure than by a visualization of success. Landry's approach has obviously worked well for many players. But not until I met Coach Miller did I see the power of positive motivation. He set out to know me as a person, to put himself inside me, and then to try to draw something from my talent. It's something like my personal life before and after being a committed Christian. I lived it up pretty well in the old days, taking what came, enjoying it, and forgetting about it. At the time, I thought I was enjoying that way of life. But you never know what you enjoy until you can compare it with something else. I discovered that I wasn't having much fun, after all. It just so happened that my discovery of the joy of a Christian life coincided with my coming to Denver and meeting Coach Miller. In him, too, I found that there was a far better way of coaching—at least as far as my personality was concerned.

Red drew the best out of us, I believe, by allowing us to see ourselves as winners. This process is known in motivational circles as "visualization." It can work spectacularly in very well controlled experiments, such as in weight lifting, swimming, and running. It involves complete relaxation to the point at which anxieties fade away, then a conscious effort to picture the successful accomplishment of a task. If your imagination is good enough, the theory goes, your entire nervous system reacts to your *imagined* action just as if it really happened. Then, when you are required to perform that action, your body goes through the motions just as if it is repeating something it has already done. Golfers have perfected a swing by means of a similar process, a sort of self-hypnosis. I have known receivers who go up for a pass in their dreams before an important game, then tell me the same thing happened in the actual game. Every time you throw a pass, your estimate of the trajectory of the football and the speed and direction of the receiver is a form of visualization. You certainly can't calculate it!

When I say that Coach Miller induced us to see ourselves as winners, I don't mean anything as specific as putting us into a trance! He simply created the atmosphere of confidence in which any person functions at his or her best. Back in the sixth grade, when he saw himself some day as a coach, he was unconsciously creating that same sort of confidence in himself. Whether he knew it or not, from that day on he was conditioned to do things that would eventually make his dream a reality.

Red and his wife Nancy have undoubtedly communicated their expectation of success to their children, Lana and Steve. Both are college graduates, pursuing careers that were well mapped out for them. Red talks about their careers so confidently that I know those expectations must have been part of his family life for a long time. In our own home, Suzie and I have placed a plaque, given to us by our Bible study group, to remind ourselves of our motivation. Toward the end of the Book of Joshua, the prophet asks the people what gods they will serve, and says: "As for me and my house, we will serve the Lord." This message is over our front door.

Red Miller has shown his confidence in people in a rather surprising way: in his evaluation of football talent on the open market. Now, scouting has become a rather sophisticated business. In the old days, especially when the young AFL was competing with the established NFL for talent, there were some shenanigans, which bordered on kidnapping, to keep the players drafted for one league from jumping to the other. The story is told about how the Kansas City Chiefs spread $25,000 in dollar bills on a hotel-room floor to open Gale Sayers' eyes to the beauties of a Chiefs' contract, but of course we know he resisted and went to the Chicago Bears. I remember how Richard Schutte, a friend of Pete Rozelle's, convinced me that the NFL was the right league, when a lot of money was being bandied about by the upstart league. In those days, the "big name" picks were critical to the box office as well as to the playing field. As a result, scouting for free agents was hit and miss. Today, with the precarious balance of contenders in every division, no team can afford to read the headlines alone and ignore the players who fail to make the draft.

Coach Miller likes to quote the statistic that only 2 percent of players who sign free-agent contracts wind up making the team. Yet in the winter of 1979–80 Denver had eighteen players on its roster who came to the team as free agents— easily the most in the league. This can only mean that the Broncos have been especially receptive to unpublicized talent. In contrast, 92 percent of first-round draft choices wind up on the roster, and by the fifth round about half make it. But a team like the San Francisco Forty-Niners chose to give up its number two spot in the draft in 1980 for two later picks in the first round: they were looking for solid choices rather than one big star. As this trend continues, Denver's attitude toward the handling of personnel looks impressive, indeed.

"Quality—the type of player—is important," says Miller. "Denver has built an image of the all-out player, the one who hustles, throws himself, gives everything." The speed-weight factor, the college record, the injury history still figure heavily. But motivation has become as valid as the numbers.

Red Miller remembers that day in Pittsburgh when, as he freely admitted at the time, we were "outcoached" and "embarrassed in front of a lot of people." He thinks about the people who watch the game as well as the people who pay his salary. He wants men on his side who don't give up when a Terry Bradshaw and a Chuck Noll have everything working for them. He wants players on his side who are embarrassed by not giving their best, and who can admit when they are outplayed. And who can accept being fired.

Red has given more of himself to his players than perhaps even he realizes. And this is what it means to believe in people: to be willing to share oneself with them. In *The Art of Loving*, Erich Fromm writes:

> *What does one person give to another? ... He gives him of that which is alive in him; he gives him of his*

*joy, of his interest, of his understanding, of his knowl-
edge, of his humor, of his sadness—of all expressions
and manifestations of that which is alive in him. In
thus giving of his life, he enriches the other person, he
enhances the other's sense of aliveness by enhancing
his own sense of aliveness. He does not give in order to
receive; giving is in itself exquisite joy.... Giving
implies to make the other person a giver also and they
both share in the joy of what they have brought to life.*

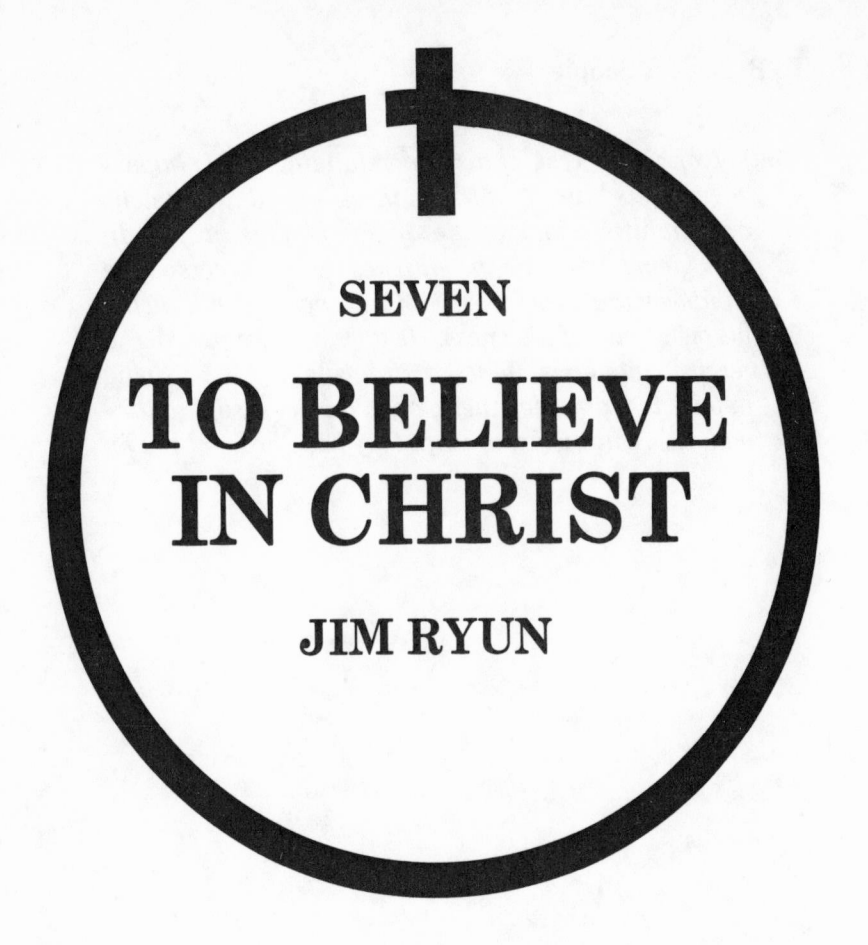

SEVEN

TO BELIEVE
IN CHRIST

JIM RYUN

For a runner, Super Bowls come only every four years. Like presidential hopefuls, track stars mark out their lives in bunches of four: 1964, 1968, 1972, 1976, 1980. For those are election years in national politics and they are also the years of the Olympics. Followers of politicians and of runners remember events by whether they came before or after one of those quadrennial milestones.

For Jim Ryun, 1972 was Munich, and it was a milestone in far more than his running career. He had set the world record for the mile six years earlier—a blazing 3:51.3 at the University of California at Berkeley that knocked an unbelievable 2.3 seconds off Michel Jazy's short-lived world standard. The next year, he took another two tenths of a second off his own record. Yet a gold medal in the Olympics continued to

elude him; Kipchoge Keino withstood his famous kick to win at
Mexico City in 1968. He began to receive hate mail, because
the world record holder is supposed to *win* for his country, not
take second place. Then he disappeared from public view and
began to win races again, and no one approached his world
mark. But when 1972 rolled around, Olympic fever again
thrust him into the center ring.

The Olympic trials were to be held in Eugene, Oregon
that year—that was the first ticket on the long road toward the
mirage of Olympic gold. And before that were the traditional
track meets to winnow out the hopefuls, and perhaps dash the
hopes of the favorites. But Ryun was the holder of the world
record: what had he to fear?

Seeking refuge from the pressure and publicity of his
native Kansas, Jim and his wife Anne and their new baby,
Heather, moved to Oregon to build their life around running.
He increased his mileage to more than a hundred a week, the
training of a marathoner. Since his high school days he had
never been a stranger to discipline and the determination that
shut everything else out of his life. He reentered the world of
international track with a reasonable 4:06 win over his archrival Keino in Los Angeles. A few weeks later he slipped to
fourth in a disappointing 4:11. He felt drained; he was working
too hard. In March, a nationally televised meet was set for Los
Angeles, and the promoters, as always, were hoping for
another battle between the two rivals and perhaps a world
record. Jim had many friends in California, the site of his early
triumphs since the day he had been the first high schooler to
break the four-minute mile. But the race began disastrously
for Jim as he tried to hurry his pace, and while his family and
twenty million Americans looked on unbelievingly he finished
dead last in 4:19.2. His world record was almost a half a
minute faster!

"I felt so tired of everything," he told reporters. "I've
never caved in in races before. I don't know what's happening." In desperation he turned to the scene of his youthful
triumphs—he was now a mature twenty-five—and to his longtime coach, Bob Timmons.

Timmons had been the coach at Wichita East High when

a spindly James Ryun had turned out for track as a sopho-
more. Fifteen years old, working morning and night delivering
papers to help his family make ends meet, he ran his first mile
in 5:38. A middle-aged jogger can work down to that time nowadays—but this was 1962, long before the era of the jogger.
Under the watchful eye of the methodical Timmons, Jim had
improved to 4:07.8 in less than a year. That was a faster time
than the great Paavo Nurmi attained in his lifetime.

Timmons was pleased to have his protégé back. He set
out to analyze what had gone wrong with his long time friend,
his *wunderkind*. There have been perhaps few other prodigies
in all of sports history like these three: Jesse Owens, Glenn
Cunningham, and Ryun. Each, at seventeen years of age, shattered some sort of world mark that only adults were supposed
to challenge. Owens took one long leap and broke the world
record for the broad jump (now long jump) at well over
twenty-seven feet, some two feet better than the existing
mark. To prove it wasn't a fluke, he came close to the same
mark in his memorable performance at the Berlin Olympics in
1936. That record stood for thirty-six years—till the Mexico
City Olympics of 1968. Cunningham set an indoor mile mark
in 1933 that would last for twenty-two years, broken only by
his own times—and then Wes Santee, his fellow Kansan,
lowered it by only six tenths of a second. It was rumored for
years, and recently confirmed by Glenn, as we have seen, that
he also broke the four-minute mile when he was in high school,
some twenty years before Roger Bannister. Ryun's prodigious
marks were *officially* recorded, and occurred in an era when
everyone was so well trained that it was not thought possible
that a youngster could compete with mature athletes. When
the great New Zealander Peter Snell, gold medalist at Mel-
bourne, was pitted against Ryun in the AAU championships in
1965, he told reporters, "I resent having anybody that young
in my kind of race." Ryun was eighteen; Ryun won. To have
been privileged to coach this prodigy was Timmons's claim to
fame, so that now, when Jim came back to him after a sojourn
in Oregon and California, it was a call to greatness.

By his own admission, Ryun was defeated, down, done
for. But the return to Kansas immediately buoyed his spirits.

Bob Timmons had watched him from afar. He had noticed that Jim had become too casual in his attitude toward meets. Jim would take off his sweats and hand them to Anne in the midfield of the track before his warmups. But track, as Jim would learn later, is a jealous lover; wife and family and friends could not enter the stadium. So as Bob welcomed Jim back to his familiar haunts he also convinced him that he couldn't expect to concentrate with a family around. From now on he would travel alone, or at least he would train in solitude and enter the stadium with all distractions behind him. The Olympic trials at Eugene were only two months away, and there was work to be done.

An AAU meet in Philadelphia gave Jim a chance to see how he was doing. Not too well: he was far back of the leaders at 4:14.2. Eugene was six weeks away. The national newsweeklies were beginning to call him the "riddle" of track and field. Jim worked harder on "interval" training, a technique that is quite common with distance runners today, but which he had favored since his college days: numerous sprints interspersed with walking, sometimes twenty quarter-miles at sixty seconds with two-hundred-yard walks or jogs in between. Long before his time, Paavo Nurmi had practiced the same technique in the forests of Finland. And Timmons put the "clock" back in Jim's head. Since a teenage accident, Jim had lost fifty percent of his hearing in one ear; even without that handicap, runners have a difficult time keeping time. "Usually you're in another world when you're in a race," Ryun says. "The timer yells out 'fifty-seven' or 'fifty-eight' and you don't respond to it until you've run another hundred yards or so. In a race, your thoughts are seldom consecutive." Oxygen demands on the legs deprive the brain of its needs. So Timmons concentrated on timing every 110 yards, or quarter of the track, until Ryun could tell how fast he was going without hearing the timer at all.

In early July 1972 Jim raised his arms in an uncharacteristic victory signal twenty yards before the finish of the U. S. Olympic trials: he was an easy winner. Next stop: Munich. But, as Jim says, God has a habit of always putting something in your path. Going back through Kansas, Jim and Anne decided to visit old friends from their college days. Anne had been a cheerleader at the university, whose football coach was Bernie Taylor. When the Ryuns stopped to visit the Taylors, they found a remarkable change in their college buddies. Clare and Bernie quietly announced that they were now Christians in a deeper sense than they had been before. The only word they could find to describe it simply was "born again." The Ryuns and the Taylors respected each others' intellectual integrity. Jim and Anne wanted to know what this new religious experience entailed.

So it happened that two months before the 1972 Olympics the Ryuns began to think about life and running and winning in terms of Christianity. Not that either Jim or Anne had strayed from the fold; from his first contact with the press Jim had always been depicted as the shy young man who went to church twice on Sundays and prayed for the other competitors. Now they began to sense, in contrast to the "witness" of the Taylors, how their own lives had been full of symbols and rules instead of substance. They dedicated their trip to Munich to the glory of God, but, as Jim would tell it later, Satan is always holding out compromises. In his heart he ached for the gold medal and the prestige and commercial success it might give him. After all, he argued as if with the Grand Inquisitor, he had a family to support.

The night before the heats for the mile run Anne had a dream—a vision, she would insist. She saw her husband lying on his back on the track, writhing in pain. Was it a premonition, or that sort of "unwishful thinking" that comes from fears in the unconscious? She kept the torment to herself. Jim's mental outlook was good; he felt at peace with himself after "accepting the Lord." True, as he knew in his heart of hearts, he was a "baby Christian." It would take years for him to mature in the full knowledge of his faith, just as it had taken years for him to become a complete runner. He remembered Bob Timmons's farewell to him: "Jim and I know it's a race with himself." After two laps in the first preliminary heat, he felt poised. It was a fast field, but when it came time to kick he would be ready. With 500 meters to go, a third of the distance, something under him gave way. Without warning he and Billy

Fordjour of Ghana found themselves a tangle of arms and legs, and when the pack brushed by Billy had pitched forward onto his chest and Jim had spilled backwards. Stunned, Ryun lifted himself on his left elbow. As he has retold it a hundred times, one thought flashed through his head: "Lord, why me? After all those years I've trained. . . ." His final hopes for an Olympic victory slipping away, he staggered to his feet and gave chase, catching one, two, three runners. But it was too late.

As he walked back into the tunnel to the dressing rooms, his mind was filled with contradictions. So this was to be his first trial as a Christian! This was God's reward—or was it God's punishment? But he would not give up. He and his teammates went over the videotapes: clearly, he had been fouled. A protest could be made; he could still qualify for the finals. The American team requested "reentry" for Ryun, and supplied the tapes to the Olympic judges. The machinery of committees ground on while Jim waited, prayed. Finally the judges announced that the videotapes probably told the truth: Ryun had been fouled. But there was nothing they could do. However, Ryun would be free to compete in the Olympics four years hence. . . .

That final bit of consolation from the judges left Jim in a desperate rage. Come back in four years! They had no idea of the torment he had gone through at Tokyo, at Mexico City. Eight years of building, suffering, striving, all to be wiped away in a bureaucratic wave of the hand. He prayed. Then it came to him: forgive these people, he said, and at once peace again came over him. For the first time in his life he felt he was following in Christ's steps.

When you call the Jim Ryun Running Camps, in Santa Barbara, you're likely to get a recorded message from Jim with a request to leave your name and number, for he's on the go even when he's not running. Although he held the world's record for the mile for more consecutive years than anyone else (Paavo Nurmi eight years, two months; Gunder Hagg eight years, nine and a half months; Ryun eight years, ten months), he has never received the rewards of comparable sports heroes in this country, professional or amateur. Herbert Warren Wind calls him "the only middle distance runner in history who can be classed alongside Nurmi." Now he runs as an invited "celebrity" in 10,000-km races that have become popular with the emergence of the jogger. He endorses a running shoe and occasionally other items connected with his sport. He creates programs on a regular basis for a Christian radio station in Santa Barbara, KBLS. Although he has come a long way from Wichita and delivering newspapers, he still works a long day for his living and has achieved few goals that stack up to much in the eyes of a secular society, the eyes of the world. At the end of each recorded message, he leaves a favorite quotation from the Bible. The last time I talked with him it was: "Greater is He who is in you than he who is in the world."

Jim's fascination with the historical Christ permeates everything he does. Generation after generation, millions of people read the story of Jesus, debate His teachings, argue over His importance as a prophet, a martyr, a religious leader. Surprisingly few are able to *see* Christ; for that matter, surprisingly few see their own fathers or their own mothers. Our vision of the historical Christ is colored and clouded by many layers of the diffuse light of history. He was most certainly a Jew, but our pictures of Him throughout the Middle Ages, the Renaissance, and our own 'scientific' era are of a northern European, with flowing, light brown hair, high cheekbones, delicate lips, even blue eyes. He appears to move majestically across the dusty Palestinian landscape without ruffling his tunic or scuffing a sandal. He does not sweat, cry, laugh, or show much emotion of any kind until His last days. He is stern, sometimes impatient, but always, like an idealized father figure, self-controlled to the point of being a bore.

How different a view we get if we actually read the Bible instead of trusting the secondhand sources and the preconceived opinions that spring from pious art. In recent years, filmmakers have moved beyond the stereotypes of movies like *King of Kings* to give us the man, warts and all. Pasolini's *The Gospel According to St. Matthew* portrays a rebel hurling challenge after challenge to the self-righteous fat cats of the ruling orthodoxy. A few years ago, a British actor, Alec McCowen, thought the exact text of the Gospel according to Mark might make a good play. Though not a churchgoer, he had an old Bible on his bookshelf that had been given to him when he was seven years old by a Sunday-school teacher. He had read only excerpts from it over the years, but one day it took hold of him. "I started memorizing the text as a hobby, as an experiment. I kept asking myself, 'How can you do this in the sense that you are going to charge admission?' I kept the whole thing a secret at first. When I finally told people I was learning St. Mark, the reaction was total disbelief and horror. I imagine they had never bothered to read it." McCowen's one-man play had an extended run in London, then on Broadway, and finally toured the United States. Confronted with the instant success of the play (without calls of "author! author!"), the actor could only assume that the same sense of story appealed to his audiences that originally had appealed to him. The figure of Christ is real and His message has power without any embroidery. That simple fact frequently is lost for the ordinary reader in the maelstrom of theological interpretation that is the unfortunate legacy of religious divisions.

Is Christ divine? On the one hand, the nonbeliever takes this to be a meaningless question, since there is no divine for him, certainly not any man. On the other hand, the believer easily falls into the habit of seeing nothing *but* divinity in Christ. Jesus is bullet-proof, tear-proof, and sex-proof. Oh yes, He suffered and died. Sure, He cried when His friend Lazarus was reported to have died and when He thought about the fate of Jerusalem. And yes, He associated with prostitutes, and preferred the Mary who talked with Him to the Martha who busied herself with chores in the kitchen. The trouble with seeing Christ as God with clothes on is that He becomes a sort of supersaint or magic spirit who can never be a model for us mortals. In fact, after making Him a pure spirit the next step is to idealize Him as a vision and pretty soon wish Him away as a nice symbol.

His mother and father have suffered a similar fate, a kind of canonization by association. Joseph is little more to us than pictures on holy cards, the original long-suffering laborer. Yet in the little village of Nazareth where Jesus grew up, a major thoroughfare of Middle Eastern commerce ran close by Joseph's door. There, in the dust of caravans, the swearing of merchants, and the sweat of artisans, Joseph and his son must have learned a lot about the politics and economics of the day, must have traded and argued with real people. The question of Mary in theological speculation is a more delicate matter, except that she holds a position of reverence in all Christian sects. This is where Jim Ryun echoes a sentiment with which I heartily agree: that the message of Christ is too important in itself to be watered down by doctrinal differences over the role of Mary, the existence and impact of the Holy Spirit, the meaning of miracles, or a whole list of peripheral practices, such as "speaking in tongues." I'm hardly a biblical scholar, and this is hardly a theological text; my feelings might be summed up by a curious statement from an unexpected source, Queen Elizabeth I: "There is only one Christ Jesus and one faith; the rest is a dispute about trifles."

Jim Ryun's ability to identify with Christ, to find the real Jesus there between the lines of the familiar gospels that seem such a fairy tale to nonbelievers, may have been intensified by an aptitude Jim learned when quite young. He was an amateur photographer in high school. He became so proficient that even though he was a shy young man he asked for and got the assignment of covering the Kansas City Chiefs for the *Wichita Capitol Journal.* One of his photos, of the great running back Mike Garrett, in fact won a prize in a statewide contest. Jim continues to mix photography with running as a hobby, explaining:

> *Photography is rather similar to running a race. The*
> *big thing is previsualization. Besides having a clear*
> *idea of what you're after, to be really good, I think, you*
> *must have a dream and a hope.*

There is the essence of motivation: not only to see yourself winning a race or completing a pass, but to put everything else in your preparation that adds up to "a dream and a hope." To believe in Christ is also to want desperately to know Him, to trust Him, to be like Him. For belief is nothing if it is only a mental acquiescence, an intellectual commitment. How obvious, but how hard to see!

The psychologist and sociologist Robert Coles says this more forcefully in the larger context of a critique of modern secular society:

> *We possess no larger, compelling vision that is worth any commitment of energy and time. . . . We shun the elderly, reminders of our own mortality. We worship super-athletes, promoted by endless and sometimes corrupt schemes. We cultivate postures—ironic cynicism, skeptical distance—meant to keep us from the inevitable difficulties of human involvement. We play it cool, play it fast, and, in the clutch, place our faith in lotions and powders and soaps and dyes and surgical procedures so that we can stay—we hope, we pray—in the game as long as possible, playing at life, because from the outside (society) we have every encouragement to do so and from the inside (family life) we have also learned that such a way of getting along is desirable.*

Those who do not believe in something larger than life place their faith, by default, in "playing at life." The danger, according to Jim, is always the temptation to dilute our beliefs, to compromise. He consciously asks himself such things as, "Would Christ go to that movie?" "Would the Lord endorse that product?" Not too long ago Jim was asked to participate in a TV commercial for a light beer. Now, Christ turned water into wine, not Kool-Aid, at the wedding feast at Cana. And at the last supper he asked to be remembered in the eating of bread and the drinking of wine. But Jim literally asked himself, "Would Christ be a part of this sort of promotion of a beverage, if he had to make a living and support a family like mine?" He didn't have to wait for the answer—and, incidentally, Jim's brood now consists of Drew and Ned and Catharine in addition to Heather.

Early in his career, Ryun learned something about the "worship of super-athletes, promoted by endless and sometimes corrupt schemes." At first sports offered only the chance to earn a little recognition—a letter on the high school track team, which he thought, like all young men, would get him the attention of a certain young lady. (It didn't, he confesses.)

When he became a standout, vanquishing every other high
school miler in Kansas, his taste for recognition grew like a
drug. And race promoters fed on that taste. He soon found out
that some of them would take one of the favorites aside, slip
him some traveling money, and ask him to set an impossible
pace: anything to hype the crowd, and all in the name of setting
new records. On one occasion Jim and a friend, who had been
approached with such a proposition, decided to waltz through
the mile at a 4:30 pace, just for spite; but at the last minute
they couldn't bring themselves down to the same level as the
race organizers. On the international scene, some years later,
he discovered that athletes had a ruthless code of their own,
which included intentional spiking and under-the-table payments to favor certain friends. But his lifelong battle, the most
difficult of all, was to be free from the domination of sports
itself.

"Sports tolerates no rivals," he likes to quote. It is an idol
that might well have been mentioned among those God pro-
scribed in handing down the First Commandment. In Exodus
20:1–4, the words "I have liberated you from your slavery"
have a special meaning for Jim, for the slavery in his case was
clearly the ever-increasing demands of the quest for the
Olympic gold medal. The ups and downs of his career, difficult
to explain in such a superbly conditioned athlete, can be
traced to the psychological pressure placed on him by that god
of success. At his first Olympic Games, Tokyo 1964, his
publicity had preceded him. As he waited in the tunnel for the
call to the first heats, the seventeen-year-old, weakened by a
virus, conjured up fears of failure instead of hope and a dream.
"What if I bomb out?" he thought, and so he did, finishing
dead last in his first attempt. He was ready to retire from
track. Only teammate Dyrol Burleson's Dutch-uncle consoling
kept him from quitting. At the NCAA meet preliminary to the
1968 trials, Ryun veered off the track at the third lap. "Too
much competition, too many races, too much pressure," he
told the press. The public called him a "quitter" in hate mail
and letters to editors of newspapers. At the trials at Lake
Tahoe a few months later, he pulled up short in the half mile
when he fell off the pace, later explaining that he panicked at

the thought of giving an all-out effort and perhaps injuring himself for the mile. When he was safely over that hurdle and on his way to the Mexico City Olympics, he paid new obeisance to his god. "I needed a preoccupation like running," he explained; "something was missing from my life. Now it's complete." But it would not be until that tragic fall in the Munich Olympics that Jim would realize what was really missing from his life.

The life of Christ is free of compromises and as such is Jim's only sure guide to avoid compromises in his own life. He is aware of the misuses of the "born again" enthusiasm. Businessmen tell him they achieve success through the power of Christianity, or that they keep their jobs through the "positive" outlook that their religion gives them. Christ answered, "Not everyone who says to me 'Lord, Lord' shall enter the kingdom of heaven." The joy of believing in Christ is the joy of freedom—from all the other gods that lay claim to one's soul. Jim and Anne communicate that joy to the seventy or more young people who attend each of their running camps, not by proselytizing, but by making the message of the gospels available in skits, songs, and readings for all who want to take the time to take them in. When he retired from competitive running in 1976 to devote full time to his "running with Christ" activities, he at last received some sympathetic treatment from the press. "Most of the reporters at the press conference expressed sorrow that I was leaving something I had given so much of my life to," he says. "But I didn't have a bit of sorrow. I was thinking how much better the future would be."

Who, then, is this Christ that Jim Ryun knows so well, and who has brought such peace and joy into his life? How can we know Him as more than another prophet, a wise man, a reformer with a lasting message of love? After all, how much do we know of His contemporaries, or even of great moral leaders of more recent times? I once knew a man who said, "I don't know Christ, and I don't need to know any such person." Then someone read to him some verses from Matthew 25:

Come, you blessed of my father, inherit the kingdom prepared for you from the foundation of the world. For

I was hungry and you gave me food; I was thirsty and
you gave me drink; I was a stranger and you took me
in. I was naked and you clothed me; I was sick and
you visited me; I was in prison and you came to
me. . . .

The spirit of Christ lives in every man and woman, if you
believe the words of the Christ depicted in the Gospels. To
everyone who says he can't get beyond the words, the history
books, the theological discussions, or the Sunday school
images, Christ answers that He is as close as the next person.
No, more: in His divinity He *is* the next person. For when a
man asks:

Lord, when did we see you hungry and feed you, or
thirsty and give you drink? When did we see you a
stranger and take you in, or naked and clothe you? Or
when did we see you sick, or in prison, and come to see
you?

The answer Christ gives is direct beyond any possibility of
confusion or uncertainty:

Assuredly, I say to you, inasmuch as you have done it
to one of the least of these my brothers or sisters, you
have done it to me.

The divine spark that is in every person is what makes all life
sacred, all human beings worthy of respect. So if you happen
to call Jim Ryun and get the recorded message that is one of
his favorites, you'll know what he has in mind: Greater is He
who is in you than he who is in the world.

Quarterbacks are measured by stamina and poise as much
as by their completion records, and Terry Bradshaw is the current
standard of comparison in the NFL. He throws the ball like a

javelin—he once held the high school record for that, too—but he is equally respected as the leader on the field, of the toughest team in the business.

Jim Zorn has brought a different style to the game—as different as Seattle is from Pittsburgh. The first of a new generation of quarterbacks, Jim's zest for the pure game

radiates throughout the exciting Seahawks. "Whatever you do, do heartily for the Lord" is the watchword of the Christian athlete in a secular world.

A second sense develops between quarterback and receiver. In this sequence from a Denver-Kansas City game, one can sense the ballet-like patterns in which both passer and receiver are engulfed. A Morton to Dolbin pass connects under

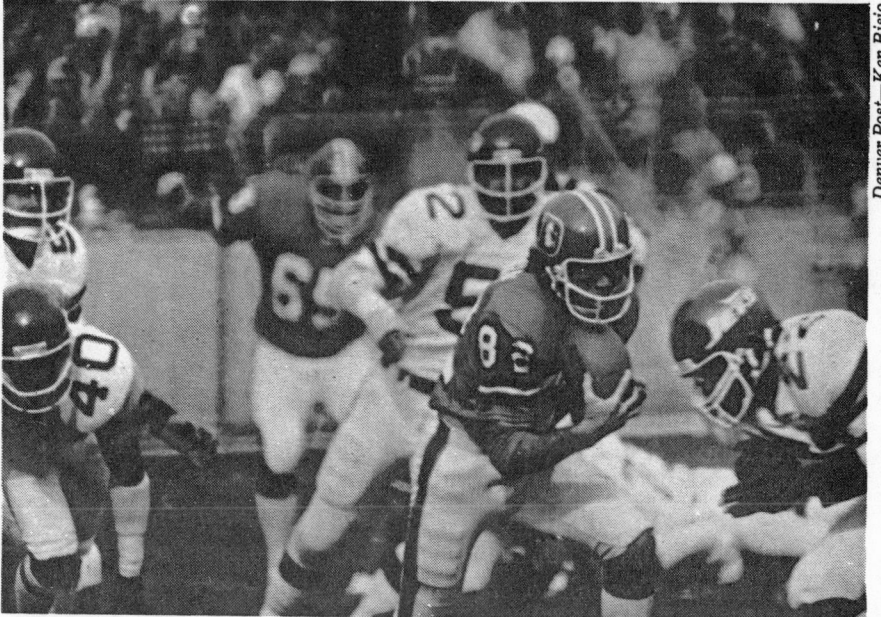

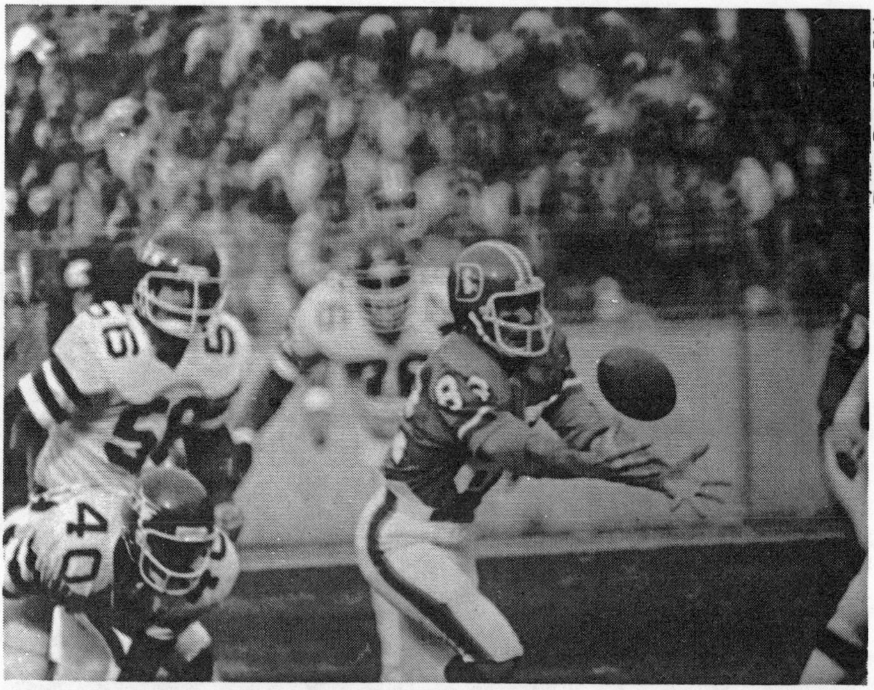

Denver Post—Ken Bisio

Denver Post—Ken Bisio

pressure; neither man can see the other during most of the sequence, but both make adjustments as the play develops from their understanding of how the other reacts.

Denver Post—Ken Bisio

Coach and quarterback share a special relationship on most teams. They work so closely on offensive strategy, their lives become intertwined on and off the field: Bradshaw and

Noll, Zorn and Patera, Staubach and Landry, Morton and
Miller. Coaches fire the enthusiasm of the whole team, and
emotions are shared throughout the organization.

As the scoreboard tells the story of Denver's triumphant 1977 season, quarterback and Bronco general manager, Fred Gerhke, react to the intensity of the moment. Red Miller is

carried off the field as 70,000 fans stay in their seats in the Mile High Stadium to celebrate the AFC championship and their first taste of the Super Bowl.

Denver Post—Ken Bisio

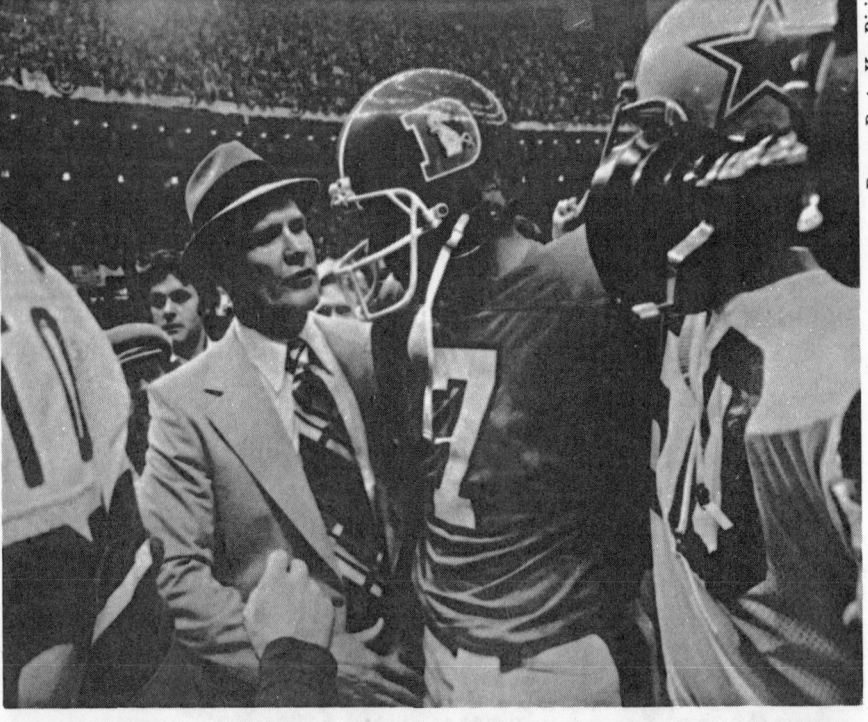

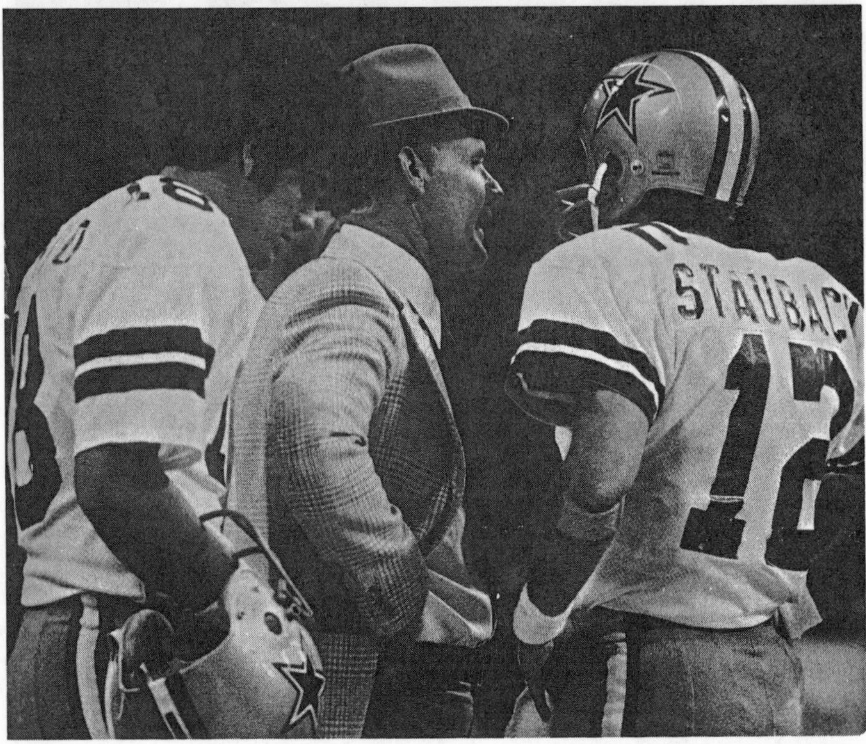

© 1978 Bukki Erwin

And when Dallas demolishes the Broncos' dream of a
world championship, Tom Landry is the first Cowboy with a
comforting word for the losing quarterback—they have shared
that moment many times in the dozen years they have known
each other. The retirement of Roger Staubach has ended the
most visible partnership in pro football, one that the fans of
every team will miss. The quiet integrity of both men, their
Christian witness by example and word, has given a new
dimension to the game. For this, as much as his heroic deeds on
the field, Roger will always be America's favorite quarterback. His
ability to rally against impossible odds—as in this final game of
the 1979 season against the Redskins—is the mark of greatness.

Fans seldom know what their favorite coaches or players
did before, during, or after their exploits in the NFL. . . . That

Tom Landry was a high-stepping running back in his salad days at Texas. . . . That with Alicia he has raised daughters Lisa and Kitty, and Tom, Jr. . . . That teams like the Cowboys relax together

off the field—here, in a golf tournament, Cliff Harris, Roger, and Robert Newhouse . . . or that other careers go on in the lives of their Sunday-afternoon heroes. Jack Dolbin, a chiropractor, ironically had his career short-circuited with a knee injury in

mid-season 1979. . . . That professional careers start many years earlier—here, Craig, Bruce Stephenson, and Jack Schaub at Campbell High on their way to becoming All-Americans at the University of California.

John Rawlston—News Free Press

Injuries, losses, bad luck are the everyday experiences of athletes in the demanding sport of distance running, as well as in professional football. But the dedicated athlete strives above all to excel, not to win at another's expense. The marathon epitomizes this spirit. As Bill Rodgers drives to his record-breaking finish at Boston, 1978, the strain of competition is written in his face. Just behind his right arm, a younger challenger, Jeff Wells, helps create one of the most dramatic finishes in the history of this premier event. Jeff knows the apparent contradiction of a Christian athlete training and competing to win; his audience is God, and he runs his best to create a spirit of excellence for his fellow runners as well. Jeff, who competes for Athletics West in Eugene, Oregon, congratulates Ed Leddy after a close race.

Jim Ryun has dueled with misfortune throughout his career. Though he held the world record for the mile longer than any other runner, his expectations have failed him at critical junctures. At the Munich Olympics, 1972, he was eliminated in a preliminary heat after a disastrous fall in the final lap.

At the "dream mile" in the International Freedom Games at Philadelphia in 1971, Marty Liquori edged Jim at the height of his career, sending him into a period of doubt about his objectives in life.

Fellow Kansan Glenn Cunningham, who dominated the American mile in the 1930s, has also known the agony of failed expectations—missing the gold medal in two Olympics and seeing a third canceled by war. Here, he powers to a typical fast finish to edge his perennial rival, Archie San Romani, at the AAU championships in 1937.

Glenn has dedicated his life to helping children. Here he shows off some of his own. At the Glenn Cunningham Youth Ranch near Augusta, Kansas, farm animals were an essential part of Glenn's program, caring for orphaned or abandoned children. Since this 1965 photo, the Cunninghams have moved to Arkansas, where they continue their work. The Cunninghams and their children were feted at the 1962 Seattle World's Fair.

EIGHT

TO BELIEVE IN THE FAMILY

ROGER STAUBACH

Before Spring training in 1979, I went down to Dallas to be part of a "roast" for Don Meredith at Southern Methodist University. Don was in typically fine form, assuring everyone that football doesn't build character and trying to prove it. The next day I stopped in at Roger Staubach's office on the north side of Dallas to see how things were going for my old friend and competitor. He was now president of Holloway-Staubach, real estate developers. We talked about investments in condominiums in Tucson, about the growing family, about Dandy Don's performance the night before. The president of SMU, who apparently doesn't spend much time watching *Monday Night Football,* kept referring to him as "Dandy *Dan,*" so Don adopted the name for himself—to the delight of the audience and the bemusement of the president. And there were dozens of hilarious and outrageous moments that we shared from the fraternity of professional and collegiate football greats of the past. The roast was supposed to be filmed for a later showing on television, but it never came off. TV wasn't ready for it, and I hope it never will be.

Roger had to leave his office early that day to make it out to the practice field for his daily workout—several miles of running, some weight lifting, calisthenics. "One of these days," he said, "I'm gonna wonder how to fill up my day when the Dallas Cowboys are out of my life." The thing about Roger is you never know when he's joking. He's now the father of five youngsters, from preschool to teenager, with whom he'd rather play games any day. And the Cowboys without Staubach?

Whether I knew it or not, I was competing with Roger from the day I suited up at Cal. He was scouted by every college power in the country at about the same time. The only place he wanted to go, Notre Dame, failed to make him an offer, until he played in a high school all-star game both as quarterback and free safety. Then it was too late: he had made a commitment to Annapolis. Every Catholic lad in the country must dream of playing for the Irish, but Roger already was beginning to show his mettle. Instead, he had a chance to prove himself in a better way. When the College All-Star Game rolled around four years later—in those days in midsummer— there were four quarterbacks competing for the job of playing against the world-champion Cleveland Browns. John Huarte of Notre Dame was the local favorite, since Chicago is Notre Dame territory and the game was played in Soldier Field. Against him were Bob Timberlake of Michigan, Roger, and I. Since I had been the number one draft pick of the Cowboys that year, and Roger was tenth because of his uncertain military status, we eyed each other cautiously. Otto Graham ran us through scrimmages against the Chicago Bears and picked Roger as his QB.

The Annapolis, image, the Catholic upbringing, and the crew-cut straightness of his features had already begun to convince people that Staubach was humorless and too goodie-goodie for words. It didn't matter that he hammed it up on the

Ed Sullivan show, or that he had a penchant for practical jokes, or that he had quite an eye for the girls. But Otto Graham saw the real Roger. He kept warning Roger in their workouts not to jump up to lay off passes over the heads of charging linemen. At almost six feet three inches he was big enough to stay planted and find his receivers. But it was a habit he had throughout his days at Navy, and he had suffered seventeen shoulder separations partly as a result of leaving his upper body exposed. In the second half of the All-Star game, trailing only 7–3, Staubach jumped up to avoid a blitz and his left shoulder was knocked completely out by a tackler's helmet. Recovering in the hospital, he received a printed thank-you note from the coach, at the bottom of which Otto scribbled: "I told you not to jump, Roger."

Roger's four-year tour of duty in the Navy at the height of the Vietnam War only delayed the inevitable competition we would have at Dallas. And the "Staubach of Navy" image continued to grow. He and his wife Marianne now had a daughter, Jennifer. In 1967 and 1968 he made an appearance at the Cowboys' training camp in Thousand Oaks, California, on leave, and all of us began to take notice of his potential. Meredith, who was successfully defending his number one quarterback position against me, poked fun at this hard-working, intensely serious Navy man. "Listen, we've got to do something about Staubach," he said. "He's gonna have to learn what an NFL quarterback is like. He needs to grow his hair long, start smoking, drinking, and things like that to keep up the image."

I've already told the story of our days together under Landry, our continuing friendship, and our eventual meeting on opposite sides of the field in Super Bowl XII. As we talked about real estate in his office on North Central Expressway, I felt we might have at least one more shot at each other in a game of football. But a little less than a year later, with another spring training looming, Roger was approaching one of the truly serious moments in his life. A press conference was called for a Monday morning; quarterbacks don't call press conferences to announce they expect to have a good year.

Tension was building all over the city. As *Sports Illustrated* told the story, several calls came in one morning to the Cowboys' business office, threatening to cancel season tickets if Roger was going to retire. Then Staubach called in, asking how many season-ticket holders had complained.

"Dammit, Roger," the receptionist said. "They were all *you!*"

To let himself down easy, Staubach drove out to the Cowboys' practice field the morning of the press conference and explained his decision to retire to his teammates. The story was immediately picked up by the Associated Press, and the unofficial news began to sink in around the country. Roger had once inched along a narrow ledge outside Cowboys' president Tex Schramm's skyscraper window—again as a gag—and the first comment to the press came from him: "There's not a question that Roger Staubach is this country's greatest sports hero today and maybe of our time. He is unique in that his following spans age generations. He has *been* the Cowboys for the past eleven years."

Roger wanted to avoid all this in a formal press conference, but that afternoon it came anyway. The Cowboys were "America's team," and Roger was their leader. He explained that the five concussions he received during the 1979 season weren't responsible for his decision—as the reporters put down their pencils and gave him quizzical looks. "I've never worried about injuries and the examinations I underwent showed no brain damage," he told them earnestly. He added, "One doctor was concerned that the concussions might be an accumulative thing." He then twitched his head twice, and the laughing reporters knew he had set them up again.

The risks were real, however, to his wife and family, and there were many things for him to do with his time. What if his backups at quarterback suffered injuries in the 1980 season—would he consider coming back to help out? "I'm not adverse to helping," he said cautiously. "It would depend on the circumstances." Tom Landry predicted that in an emergency Staubach would play. It was a nice thought, but both men knew the wishful thinking had to end. Roger thanked all his teammates, tempering the heavy mood of the hour with spontaneous quips. Then it came time to speak of his coach.

"Of course the nuts and bolts of the Dallas Cowboys," he said, pausing to find the words, "was the man who wears the funny hat on the sidelines." After those eleven years together, his voice cracking, the quarterback could not say his name.

The days are now gone, I hope, when a standard joke begins, "There were three men in a rowboat. One was a Catholic, one was a Protestant, and one was a Jew." Also thankfully gone are the pieties of World War II movies, when the Catholic chaplain would show his sudden rise to the heights of tolerance by performing a nondenominational service. Yet, with all the changes that have occurred in this ecumenical age, divisions of pride and custom still keep Christians apart. Staubach, who has always been a Catholic, finds this fact to be the real disgrace of Christianity—and he holds his own church responsible for much of the continuing separation of believers. Even the Jewish religion, because it considers Christ to be only one of many religious prophets, should not be considered inimical to Christian principles; for the Bible's Old Testament is basic to everything Christ taught. The Judeo-Christian tradition is a unity, not two loosely affiliated, before-and-after acts of an historical play. Christ was a Jew who wanted to enrich, not destroy, His heritage.

It's surprising to me how easily two people of differing denominations can discuss their common grounds while their churches can only discuss their differences. Roger's Catholicism runs deep. He attributes its roots to the training and especially to the example of his parents. He has studied the dogmas of his faith, knowing full well that the very word "dogmas" raises questions in many mature minds. In spite of all his familiarity with this very traditional set of beliefs, Roger is at home with any of the born-again Christians I have ever met. But why should this be surprising? I think we create within ourselves images of other believers based on fear, insecurity, or pride. How else can we explain the evident fact that many churches have been and still are prejudiced against blacks or against the poor or against foreigners?

There are many things about Catholicism that Roger admits can be a stumbling block to other Christians—and to

Jews—if they aren't put in proper perspective. As Jim Zorn once mentioned to me, he doesn't understand the need for the devotion to Mary that Catholics have traditionally practiced. Why is a mediator needed when we can go directly to Christ? Others have asked Roger why confession to a priest seems—or seemed—so necessary for Catholics. The whole hierarchy of the Catholic Church seems to many to be a self-evident human invention, designed to preserve privilege. And the claim to be the only true succession of the Apostles obviously makes other Christians feel like poor relations. Roger explains that his view of Christianity is based on more than tolerance: because human beings are so different in so many ways, they necessarily have different manifestations of their beliefs. And so there are many churches.

We keep on asking, "But what is the truth?" But we have to live from day to day, with problems so complex no computer could ever sort them out. We have to accept huge areas of reality on faith. The hypocrisy is to avoid the ethical message of Christ—what we should do, how we should behave—simply because we haven't arrived at a fully satisfactory rational explanation of Christian theology.

Since Roger's Christian stance is so well publicized, he often runs into strangers who wish to challenge his opinions. Once a young woman asked him, "When were you saved?" He answered that there was no particular day on which he felt he was saved; salvation had a different meaning to him. The woman answered, "Well, then, you're not really saved." This sort of expression of beliefs doesn't make sense to him. Lately, he says, he finds himself clamming up in such discussions because they lead nowhere.

The problem of dealing with a myriad of opinions about life and death, salvation, redemption, good and evil is insurmountable for theologians, but at least tackled in the long Christian tradition. So we have another area of faith: faith in the cumulative wisdom of previous generations. This is known as the tradition of the Church, as contrasted with the revelation we receive in the Bible. As Roger points out, faith in both sources of knowledge is a characteristic we see in great men and women of the most skeptical generations. He once went through the New Testament with a pencil, underlining each occurrence of the word "faith." It's an eye-opener.

It's obvious that Roger Staubach has accepted the Bible as one of his foundations in life. "We're all doubters," he says, "and the Apostles were at one time or another, too. The Bible is a convincing story because it makes sense. The Apostles' lives were obviously changed. Because of Christ they did remarkable things, including giving up their own lives for their work. But it's impossible to convey the effect of Christ on yourself to someone who doesn't know the Gospels or doesn't have any faith in them. To that kind of person it's all like a magic show."

In the past four or five years, Roger says, he's been studying the Bible more carefully as a member of the Cowboys' study groups. As Landry puts it, it's hard to enjoy watching football if you don't know anything about the game— the rules, the history of the teams, the duties of various positions, and so forth. For the same reason it's a bore to listen to a Bible reading on Sunday if you don't have any background to understand it.

The subject of prayer suffers from the same indifference, Roger believes. If you believe in praying, you believe in a higher being, and vice versa if your concept is of a God who is involved with the world of His creation. But to the nonbeliever, prayer is a throwback to a mythmaking, superstitious age. Roger says he finds himself praying to win a game now and then, but it's really just a heartfelt wish. When the game is over, he doesn't attribute the win or the loss to God. His beliefs aren't substitutes for his actions. Does God answer prayers? Since there is no time with God, no before or after, it doesn't make sense to think of him "answering." Protestant theologian Paul Tillich writes:

> [Believers] are aware of the paradoxical character of every prayer, of speaking to somebody to whom you cannot speak because he is not "somebody," of asking somebody of whom you cannot ask anything because he gives or does not give before you ask, of saying "thou" to somebody who is nearer to the I than the I is to itself.

This formulation comes close to expressing the mystery of Christian belief, and why it requires so much faith. It is the ultimate in humility for a man of Roger Staubach's education, self-discipline, and intelligence to seek his faith in a religion which our modern world finds so easy to ignore as a superstition.

In 1971, in Super Bowl VI, Staubach played a good game, but he felt it was a team effort that made it Dallas's first big triumph. "The sports writers didn't like Duane Thomas, or they would have voted him most valuable player," he says. "Instead, they had a safe call in giving it to me." The prize was a new car of one's choice. The story is worth repeating. Roger picked a station wagon. Quarterbacks at that age are supposed to be men about town, not family men. They're supposed to want sports cars. "Actually," Roger says, "I thought it was a darn good decision. It was just what we needed." But he has to laugh at his own naivete. He's his own best straight man. I wonder, though, if Roger picked that station wagon just as another great gag. . . .

The following season was the one he had to sit out with a shoulder separation, even though he was now following Otto Graham's advice ("I told you not to jump, Roger."). You'll recall that toward the end of that year he came in with only a couple of minutes on the clock and scored two touchdowns against the Forty-Niners to get us in the NFC championship against Washington. With about thirteen minutes of playing time against my entire season as a starter, he was then picked by Coach Landry to start against the Redskins. It was a dismal loss for us, yet Roger looked forward to the 1973 season with every expectation of beating me out again. Then a cloud came over his life. His mother, Betty, widowed about ten years previously, was found to have cancer. He brought her to his home in Dallas from the suburb of Cincinnati where the family had always lived. The doctors gave her eight or nine months to live. Marianne, who had been a nurse, prepared to make her mother-in-law's life as painless and cheerful as possible.

Roger didn't let us know the strain he was working under till much later. In training camp, however, he was as determined a man as I've ever seen; this last season he wanted for Betty. In one of our exhibition games that summer, when the starting assignment for quarterback was still in doubt,

Tom Landry and his wife offered their box at the stadium to Betty Staubach. It was a beautiful gesture, but Roger felt he had to turn it down: he wanted not the slightest suspicion of favoritism between the coach and himself. He says he regrets it now, for his mother's sake, but Betty always had a respect for her son that went far beyond football. In the end, as I've mentioned before, he wrested the starting assignment from me again. And he played brilliantly throughout a trying year, meeting the St. Louis Cardinals in two crucial games and coming up with commanding victories in both. On the Thursday before the second of those games, his mother, now reduced to a pitiful sixty pounds and in intermittent pain, died after a short coma. The funeral was in Cincinnati Saturday. The following day in St. Louis Roger played his heart out, not only nailing down the division title but winning the individual passing championship of the NFC for the second time. When I presented him with the game ball in the team meeting the following week, everyone but Roger thought it was an anticlimax. There was something that he said to me years later, after I had become a Christian, that helped me understand how he could go through that period without moping or feeling sorry for himself. He was able to kid around, even make fun of himself all through that dismal season. "I think," he said, "that Christ was really a smiler."

Roger's sense of family life and the handing down of values from one generation to the next began with his first few years in his small home in Silverton, Ohio. His grandmother on his mother's side had lived with the Staubachs since he was born. The Catholic tradition was well established in their private life as well as in churchgoing and attending parochial schools. Roger grew up knowing how hard his mother had to work—often at a full-time job to help make ends meet, later caring for her mother when she became senile. And his father suffered all through this period with a diabetic condition that would end his life prematurely. He was an only child; the impact of his elders on him was immense.

"My parents gave me something I could count on— values. The good things I have now came from them," he says. "And when I got married, I formed a bond with someone else in somewhat the same way. I was no longer rudderless. Friends of mine would ask me, 'Aren't there other things in life you'd like to experience?' and I'd say 'Sure. But my family now controls my values.' " He adds with a smile, "It's a good thing I love my wife, because if I didn't I don't know what kind of a life it would be for me!"

It's quite fashionable these days to predict the end of the family—at least the *extended* family, as we know it. And the statistics on the number of divorces and kids raised in one-parent families are awesome. Yet Roger and Marianne and their type of family are a pretty good demonstration of the idea that what things *are* is not necessarily what things *ought* to be. A trend away from family formation in the traditional style should not be assumed to be a good trend, as is often the case. In my opinion, much of the old belief in the family has been undermined by another trend that is equally complex—the growing equality of women. That's a good trend! But the mistake is to think that the family is the enemy of women. Or that the Judeo-Christian tradition thrives on the suppression of women's rights. Is it better to have a job in the commercial world (as about half of all women now do) or to have the job of raising a child? To most feminists, I'm sure, the answer would be self-evident—for the self-interest of the woman. Or would it? Consider how G. K. Chesterton once compared a teacher in a school with a teacher in the home:

> *How can it be a larger career to tell other people's children about the Rule of Three and a small career to tell one's own children about the universe? How can it be broad to be the same thing to everyone, and narrow to be everything to someone? No; a woman's function is laborious, but because it is gigantic, not because it is minute.*

Or consider a more recent comment along the same lines by novelist Doris Lessing:

> *I so much hate the way women who have children and run homes are put down all the time. Sometimes you meet a woman with four kids and you say, "What are you doing?" and she says, "Oh, I'm afraid I'm only a housewife." It's enough to make you cry when you*

> *know the work this woman does, how hard she has*
> *struggled with it all. ... Middle-aged women, at the*
> *end of half a lifetime of working with children and so*
> *forth, are the most highly equipped people there are.*
> *They can turn their hands to absolutely anything.*
> *They can cope with God knows what human situ-*
> *ations with tact and patience.*

Yes, it's easier for a man to believe in the family than for the woman who must make it work. But men are learning. They'd better.

Some ninety miles north of Houston, in a dirt yard the size of a sandlot baseball field, Roger Staubach stands in the midday sun flipping passes to Bill Glass—the former All-Pro defensive end for the Cleveland Browns. Their audience of denim-clad men, mostly black, looks on appreciatively, for they don't get many demonstrations of the professional game in prison. Roger is Bill's "warm-up man." They put on their performance at prisons throughout the Southwest as the opportunity arises, grabbing the interest of their truly captive audience through the universal appeal of football, then talking about some of the things that have motivated their own lives. Roger speaks in terms of the difference between a temporary and a permanent life; in this temporary life, he says, what counts is how we build toward the permanent one. Bill Glass has been leading his "prison crusades" for many years—without a budget or paid help of any kind. He has taken St. Paul's words seriously: "Remember the prisoners as if chained with them."

Some of the prisoners are well remembered, but only for their past days of glory. Olympic sprinter and Cowboys' receiver Bob Hayes is working his way back to respectability here, as is former Oakland Raiders' star Warren Wells. Warren talks about getting back to the street, but only with the help of his parents, who have remained solidly in his corner through an ordeal of arrests, probations, bouts with alcohol, suspensions, and divorce. The aim of Bill's program is to inspire hope—not to sell religion—the kind of hope that more fortunate young men received from their parents from the beginning.

The existence of prisons down through the centuries—virtually unchanged in their hopelessness and often destructiveness—inspires in Roger another link with the presence of the gospel message. "Their attitude toward prisoners is quite understanding, because many of the Apostles *were* prisoners during the time they contributed to the gospels or the epistles. Their compassion with prisoners is just darned believable." To be in prison is to be deprived of all the rights of a family, far more than to be shut off from society. It is to be separated from the family of man.

The believability of sentiments such as this in the New Testament is the thing that speaks to the believability of Christ. Roger Staubach's Catholic Church has changed dramatically in his lifetime, reflecting a greater emphasis on the Bible, less on such things as papal infallibility, strict observance of customs, and doodads. By focusing more on the Christ of the Gospels, Catholics have grown closer to other denominations and away from comfortable myths. Father Miles Riley writes: "The Bing Crosby and Barry Fitzgerald church is dead. Commercial television can't get enough schlocky old pseudo-religious Hollywood epics in order to sell advertising around Christmas and Easter.... [Instead] we meet a Jesus who can smile and be annoyed with frightened fishermen who refuse to believe their own eyes and ears; a Jesus who is brave and determined, tender and sensitive, fearful and frustrated, angry and compassionate." Because of this Christ, and not the one that glows in the dark on the dashboard or who is fixed in a perpetual grimace on holy cards, Roger Staubach will continue to play football. Not with the Cowboys, but with guys like Bill Glass.

When Roger finally spit out the words that ended his quest for another Super Bowl, he kidded himself about his last completion of his professional career. Down 21–19 to the Rams in the playoffs, hoping for another two-minute miracle, third and ten, he looked upfield and found everyone blanketed. So he decided to bury the ball in the turf and go for one last down. Only it sailed out of his hand straight for a tackle, Herb Scott—an ineligible receiver. Scott couldn't believe his eyes, and instinctively pulled the ball in. Another penalty. And Roger's final pass missed everyone. He commented to the deadpan press: "He's worked hard during his career, and he never got to catch one before. And he did such a good job getting open on the play."

It did happen, though, that Staubach ended the regular season on a fantastic high note. That December 16, 1979 game with Washington at the Cotton Bowl had more swings to it than Roger's backyard. For the hometown crowd it was all too ominous: two fumbles in the first eight minutes, giving the Redskins a quick ten points. Then a nicely executed Theissman pass and it was 17–0. Out came the shotgun. Roger finally got a drive going with less than five minutes in the first half, and put seven points on the board. And in his patented two-minute drill he passed to another score with nine seconds left on the clock. Then, when a charged-up Cowboy team came back on the field and promptly marched to a third touchdown, the fans settled back to savor this Christmas present.

The momentum shifted just as abruptly. From a 21–17 advantage Dallas slipped to a 21–34 deficit over the third and fourth quarters. Roger missed badly and was intercepted, and Washington began playing like the team that started the first half. With the clock running under four minutes, the Redskins coughed up the ball on the Cowboy forty-one. I've mentioned the finish from Landry's point of view; suffice it to say here that Dallas scored twice in the final 240 seconds, with Raphael Septien methodically splitting the uprights: the final was 35–34. In those final two drives Roger hit seven of ten passes from the shotgun formation. He confessed to reporters, "It was a shame somebody had to lose a game like this." I think this was the game that Roger remembered as he faced the press at his retirement announcement.

It was the first day of Holy Week. When Roger arrived home to unwind with his family, some friends stopped by to share his big moment. Among them was Cowboy middle linebacker Bob Breunig, a longtime companion of Roger's in their Bible study group. That evening, Marianne, Roger, and the five children dressed up for a special dinner at a friend's house: the first night of Passover seder. Roger wore a yarmulke.

NINE

TO BELIEVE IN YOUTH

BRUCE STEVENSON

When I was in the fifth grade, there was a teacher in the school down the street from where we lived in Campbell, California, who entered us in a touch football league and trucked all twelve of us around in his station wagon to and from the games. I started throwing the ball because nobody else seemed to have the arm for it, and a chum of mine named Jack Schaub practiced with me catching it. Between us we got the knack of running patterns—even using head fakes and "look offs" that come so naturally to kids—and pretty soon we had beaten every other team within a day's driving distance. Our teacher/driver/coach built up our courage by telling us that some day we'd be playing together in a high school champion-ship, and then we'd go on to Cal and be All-Americans, and things like that. Only, he was right. The dream came true, even the part about being All-Americans.

Going to and from classes at Berkeley, I would look up at the west facade of the Boalt Hall law school building and see this marvelous invocation by Benjamin Cardozo:

> *Here is the high emprise, the grand endeavor, the splendid possibility of achievement, to which I summon you and bid you welcome.*

The world seemed charged with hope, even for someone like me who was, after all, still playing a variation on that game of touch football we learned in Campbell.

Some twelve years later, after being bounced around the very commercial world of pro football, I had settled in at Denver and we were facing a crucial game with the Oakland Raiders. Out of the blue I heard from my grammar school teacher, who used to drive us in dozens to our games: he was coming to Denver. I now had my chance to pay him back a little. (Oh, yes, at the end of our victorious fifth-grade season, we had scraped together a few dollars and bought our coach a watch at the local pawnshop; much later we found out it stopped after about six hours.) But now I could have him as my guest in the stands behind our bench.

I wish I could report it was another moment of triumph, another fulfillment of a dream. We did, in fact, win. But my teacher told me after the game that he came away somewhat mystified by it all. The fans who surrounded him were vociferous, all right—they used every profane word in the book. And not just in referring to the Raiders, but to us as well. And to me, in particular. "They were angry," he said, "and contemptuous. Was this a release of pent-up dissatisfaction with their own lives? Or was it an extension of the Little League syndrome of parents, who become so involved with winning and losing that their children become only instruments of their own aggressive fantasies?" What had happened to my mentor, my leader? The question was, what had happened to me, that I could take the whole game of professional football without wincing—the insults, the false rivalries created by the press, the grossness of many fans?

Bruce Stevenson had remained with the young—I had grown away from the young.

None of us ever completely loses his idealism, of course. We all share in the faults and the aspirations of each other, for it's a matter of degree. Everyone who listens to that heartening command from the gospels—"Unless you become as little children, you shall not enter the kingdom of heaven"—feels down deep inside that he qualifies, more or less. Yet Bruce Stevenson is one of those rare individuals who has built his life around the young—partly by accident, partly by inclination—and so stands apart from the rest of us in the degree that the values of youth shine through him.

The arena in which I grew up with Bruce as a teacher was intensely competitive in kids' sports. Campbell was known around the world for its Little League teams. In those days, soccer was still a foreign game and baseball was king. Parents projected their own lives into their children's; they even encouraged their kids to go out for the same positions they had played in their school days. My own father was an assistant Little League coach, staying in the background, but parents of many of my friends did not. I'd rather be an umpire in a Cincinnati-Los Angeles game than in a Little League game. If you think there's strong language in professional football stadiums, try one of these sometime.

What makes the Little League syndrome so distressing is that we never give kids credit for being sensitive to their parents' slightest show of anger or meanness. When you're in professional sports, you quickly learn how *your* moods are read by the fans. If you slump your shoulders a little, sixty thousand people several hundred yards away can sense that you're discouraged. A lot of this is projection, to be sure. After Super Bowl XII, in which the Dallas defensive line "plucked me like a Thanksgiving turkey," as a national magazine put it, Cowboy tackle Harvey Martin said, "Craig knew it before the game, too. I could see the fear in his eyes during the national anthem." Actually, I had a touch of hay fever. . . . But kids see everything, feel everything, diagnose everything. Remember what Glenn Cunningham said? "You can't fool kids. If you love them, they know it instinctively."

This is why I'm not quite as worried about kids attending pro football games with their parents as Bruce is. I think kids see through the temporary aberrations of adults; they realize that swearing and vilification of players on the field end as soon as the tide turns or after they leave the stadium. And I think there is enough idealism left all the while to make up for the cynicism they see in their elders. What this adds up to is this simple proposition: *We should learn from our kids, not vice versa.*

Tom Landry once wrote about the things that adults *can* do to help bridge the chasm between the bright young generation coming up and us hidebound grownups. We can no longer claim to be more wordly wise—thanks to television, explicit films, and completely uncontrolled magazines. We can no longer count on role models or sheltered environments in the schools. In all too many cases, we can't expect a child to have two parents in the home. But, almost because of the absence of all these supports we once counted on, we can now do something quite positive: we can reach out to kids, dropping the facade of our superiority or our disinterest. We can make a virtue out of the necessity thrust on us by the failure of the traditional institutions. So Landry mentions what people like Paul Anderson, America's champion, weight lifter, have done:

> *I see him stand up in front of a group of kids, take a twenty-penny nail, drive it through two one-by-sixes with his bare hand in front of these kids, then bring up about eight of them, put them on a table and get under it and lift it off the stage. Then they listen when he tells them it takes courage to be a Christian—it's no sissy's game.*

Kids aren't used to he-men talking about Christ. That's Sunday-school stuff, pious sermons, and sickly hymns. The entertainer Bobby Vinton once suggested that the churches should hire the best musical groups, songwriters, and actors to put on their performances (if that's what the purpose of music and dramatic reading is—to grab our attention). There's not a politician in the country who doesn't have a speechwriter putting words in his mouth, Vinton argues. Why not hire the best to express the theme of the Sunday sermon in the most persuasive way? Or is the purpose of churchgoing to bore kids until they must assume that the message of Christ is a big bore, too?

I'm aware that physical prowess and good entertainment don't equate with spiritual truth. Just because Paul Anderson can drive nails with his hands doesn't mean, necessarily, that he knows anything about how to live one's life. But if this book has said anything at all, I hope it has implied that there is an element of physical courage in things like playing a hard game of football or running a marathon, and that sort of courage is not too different from the strength of will it takes to face other things in life. The courage to do anything well—whether it's singing or delivering a sermon or teaching touch football—is a transferable quality. And kids know it and respect it.

There's not a quarterback I know who hasn't been side-lined more than once with a serious injury. Some have had more bad luck, or less protection from their teammates, than others. Some must be accident prone, like Lynn Dickey of the Green Bay Packers. After nine seasons, from the time he entered the league as a rookie at twenty-one, he's thrown fewer passes than Fran Tarkenton used to throw in one. He's had broken hips, separated shoulders, broken legs. Knowing this is his job, at a fairly good salary by any standard, he's forced himself to fight for starting assignments, healed or not healed. The Packers aren't slave drivers—nor is any club callous to the health of its players. But physical well-being is a precarious and subjective matter. When should one "play hurt," and when should one rest to allow the body to heal? Runners face this dilemma almost daily, for no muscle builds up without first breaking down.

Dan Lauck writes eloquently of Lynn Dickey's brand of courage, and brings to a head the question of how much physical stress is allowable in any sport—and how much kids should be encouraged to push themselves. When Dickey first came to Green Bay, Charley Johnson was the Packers' quarter-back, a veteran at thirty-two years of age. Dickey remembers: "He had six or seven scars all over his knees and shoulders. I took one look at him and I thought, 'You've had enough, pardner.' " Now Dickey sees the rookies looking at him the same way. Lauck reports:

> *His body is a sight. The scar on his right shoulder, where they rejoined his throwing apparatus, tightening it down with a screw, seems insignificant by comparison. It's only a few inches long. The scar from the hip surgery runs 14 or 15 inches, angling down and across his left hip. His left leg is worse. It is still terribly discolored. The scar is not the scalpel-thin reminder of the surgeon, but crooked and thick from the break. So some of his teammates stare, when they think he's not looking. . . .*

Limp or not, Dickey struggled through a lot of the 1979 season, because his arm was still the finest in the club. Who is to tell him it's not worth the pain? Who is to say that critics of pro football aren't right when they point to the heavy use of pain killers to "allow" injured players to stay in the game? I say it's up to the athlete himself to make the decision. Like Roger Staubach, they have to decide when the risk is too great for what they have already gained. In looking at pro football, remember, you're looking at only a small, maverick sample of American males. More leave the game early than stick around. Football players have ample opportunity during high school and college to decide for themselves if the physical demands are equal to the rewards.

Bruce Stevenson played his high school football in Burlingame, California. He remembers his coach, Bob Herwig, saying he wanted to hear a loud crash when the blocks and tackles were laid on and the pads popped. He went on to Whitworth College, had some teeth knocked out, and decided that was enough for him. That was thirty years ago. To this day he feels the character-building aspect of football is a sham, at least at the professional level. He sees the game as pure show business, with no loyalty either by the fans to the players or vice versa. As I say, Bruce has remained close to the idealism of youth and perhaps I've moved too far away from it. There's room for difference of opinion on a subject this big.

When Bruce entered teaching at the tender age of twenty-two, salaries in the profession were much farther out of line with other jobs than they are now. A teacher had to want something in this line of work very badly to sacrifice his personal welfare for it. In order to make ends meet in his newly started family, Bruce had to take whatever odd jobs there were in his off hours: for the local recreation department, in counseling, and so forth. But there was a bonus in this necessity that Bruce says he hadn't counted on and couldn't have received any other way: he became very close to every kid he came in touch with. He was hooked. He spent his weekends driving kids to games, supervising playing grounds, patching up their cuts and bruises. He took them to their homes and picked them up there, observing what kind of lives they were living. Often he took some of them into his own home—for there were many families in his community that were falling apart.

The closeness that Bruce experienced with the first kids he met in his teaching career became synonymous with his job. When "his" kids went on through grammar school to high school, they tended to drift back on weekends for more serious talks about how they were getting on. The problems were the usual ones: studies, family conflicts, sex, honesty, ambitions, sports. Bruce realized he had taken the ultimate risk—far more dangerous than the risk of physical injury. He had risked his personal involvement in the lives of young people. It was during this period that Bruce became personally involved with Sharon, Sandy, and their older brother, Craig. The Morton family would never be the same.

Bruce had to have an understanding and sensitive family to embark on such an adventure. Once a young Mexican boy— a Chicano, we would now call him—arrived in Bruce's school in the middle of the term without any visible means of support. He was hard, tight-lipped, but the story finally came out that he had been abandoned by his family in Oxnard, and had used all his money to take a bus as far as the fare would go. And so he landed on Bruce's doorstep. The Stevensons took him into their home. Now a principal, Bruce was able to help the young boy through his first few troubled years and eventually into high school. By now he had found a permanent home, but continued to accompany the Stevensons on trips to San Francisco parks and museums as one of the family. When he got his driver's license, Bruce agreed to lend him his car for a trip back to Southern California to visit his family. There was a minor traffic accident, and in the police investigation a gun was found in the car. So Bruce took it upon himself to bail him out and retrieve his car. "The price of involvement is not as great as you might think," he says, "in terms of *dollars.*" His young friend was the first in a family of seven to finish high school; many others who came his way were not so lucky.

Whenever I get back to the Bay Area, for a game with the Raiders or Forty-Niners, for a class reunion, I try to visit my friends there, especially the Stevensons. I still feel very much a part of their lives. And I wonder how many youngsters growing up today will have a chance to latch on to a Bruce Stevenson when they need him.

Bruce tells me that in the quarter century or more that he has been involved in teaching, the need for involvement has grown instead of remaining constant. Today about half of the kids he deals with as school principal are from single-parent homes. It can happen that a one-parent family does better by a child than some two-parent families, but the odds alone are against it. And while this social phenomenon has overtaken us, pressures on the teaching profession have strained their relations with children, too. Teachers entering the field are more subject oriented than child oriented, as Bruce explains it. They're now more interested in advancing their careers. The satisfaction of being a part of a child's growth is no longer enough to motivate the most dedicated teacher. Why? A dwindling school population? Greater job pressures? Lack of support from society at large? Greater reliance on government to "buy" social solutions? Perhaps all of these. But I would also guess that not enough of them get "hooked," as Bruce Stevenson did.

Adults can learn idealism from kids, but they have to take the first step.

Fritz Kreisler was embarking on an exciting career as a violinist and composer in New York City when the First World War broke out and changed his plans. He had been a musical prodigy before turning his attention to getting a medical degree, and music was what he had come back to. But now his native land, Austria, needed his medical services; he sailed for Europe and enlisted. Kreisler was spared the fate of many another idealistic youth, but was seriously wounded. He returned to New York to recuperate, and a concert was arranged at the Metropolitan Opera House to honor his interrupted career. A packed house watched expectantly as Kreisler made his appearance, slowly dragging his injured leg in a pronounced limp to the center of the stage. The applause grew as the frail figure raised his violin to start his performance. He waited, but the noise was now deafening. Though everyone had read of the young man's heroic act, and knew he had been seriously injured, his physical appearance before the audience inspired an outpouring of emotion. As much as he raised his hand for quiet, they would not let him play. It was perhaps the most sustained ovation in the history of the Met.

Do we still respond to the idealism of youth? I think so, even though the noblest example of our time—the Peace Corps—has moved off the center stage of our attention. As a nation, we are tempted these days to consider young people as another category of social problem—like the "problem" of the aged, of minorities, of mothers who have raised families and are unsatisfied remaining in the home from nine to five. But the only way we can respond fully to the promise of young people is to go out and see them: not read about them—see them in action. Perhaps then our applause for them would not be so tempered.

Bruce Stevenson has given me the opportunity to talk to many young people over the years. I guess he thinks I owe some dues. When I was with the Cowboys in Dallas, I remember hopping a plane several times in the off-season to be at a presentation of awards or to talk to a boys' club. Once I was able to visit a young admirer of the Cowboys in a small town outside Dallas, where he was dying of cancer. Believe me, I was overcome with emotion.

At the time I was hardly living a Christian life. I knew that Bruce was a believer; he acted the part. But he preferred not to talk about his beliefs except in a one-on-one situation, and then only when he thought his beliefs might be of some help to a youngster. He doesn't promote just for the sake of promoting. "Whether it helps to talk publicly about Christ is open to question," he says, knowing full well the command of the gospels to "go forth and teach all nations," and not to hide one's lamp under the table. Bruce means it's his way, with the people he usually deals with—namely, kids. For every personality there is an appropriate way of sharing what that person has to offer. For Bruce, it's a very personal thing. Over my entire playing career, up to my joining the Broncos, Bruce never made an effort to interest me in his Christian outlook. We talked about a lot of serious subjects, but he backed up his points with examples and not with biblical quotations. He had a sense of knowing what might turn me off.

When I announced my wedding in 1977, I was happy to hear that Bruce and his wife would be able to make it. After the excitement of the Pittsburgh game, the ceremony in Dallas, and a crowded reception had died down, we got away for a moment to talk. He asked what was new in my life, and I told him it was my commitment to Jesus Christ. Later, as my wife and I were opening our presents, we came upon a Bible. It was from the Stevensons.

In May of every year the professional football teams of the NFL express their own form of belief in youth by drafting college seniors into their ranks. This has become quite a sophisticated affair, although many fans might think their own teams are bereft of reason on that fateful day. There are two major scouting organizations, United Scouting and Blesto 9, that are employed by the pros to sift information on virtually every college player with varsity time in the nation. Offensive standouts, such as quarterbacks and running backs, tend to take the limelight: they are the home-run hitters of football. Even so, as we will see in the case of Jim Zorn, future stars are easily overlooked. The reason: the human factor. Desire. Persistence. Self-confidence. The Houston Oilers did quite well in 1979, becoming a playoff team on the sheer strength of their top draft choices, notably Earl Campbell. Their chief scout,

Joe Wolley, says, "We want somebody who'll suck it up and go after 'em in the fourth quarter when we're down 21–7. The young man who's got that kind of enthusiasm is the one who hits every time the ball's snapped whether it's practice or not." Youth has been measured and boxed for shipment.

One of Bruce Stevenson's concerns is the way professionalism throughout our society has diluted the idealism of the young. "Professionalism" is a polite word for it; it's the placing of a material value on everything. Everything becomes merchandise, even a man's name. Dr. John Hezel of the Oregon Medical Association recently protested the endorsement of chewing tobacco by professional athletes, on the grounds that such endorsements have become powerfully out of proportion to reality. The best known running authority in the country has lent his name to sugared cereal products that are of doubtful nutritional value to growing children. The effects of athletes' names on aspiring athletes—kids—is not hard to imagine. Dr. Hezel comments, "If Earl Campbell said he sucked on rabbit pellets, I'm sure there'd be ten thousand rabbit hutches built overnight."

Bruce has observed a sort of professionalism growing right in the schools—an attitude of "What's in it for me?" If the kids are trying to size up a baseball program, they want to know if there's an all-star team in the league. What do the uniforms look like? Who covers them in the local papers? It's not hard to see that much of this comes right off the sports pages. Bruce's point is not that everything's going to hell. The problem is that the focus is more and more on the top athletes. The star pulls the school up by his own bootstraps. "We should be moving in the direction of giving more and more kids some form of recognition," he says. "Instead, we're sending kids to a kind of high school Super Bowl with all our honors and awards. And athletic scholarships rule the roost openly at the college level. The good athletes will always take care of themselves, without our help at an early age. We should spread our compliments and our cash around."

My life has been so intertwined with Bruce's that I can't imagine what might have happened to me if I hadn't had the lucky accident of growing up in his school, at that innocent time when star quarterbacks were sports heroes and not businessmen with million-dollar contracts. Sports used to be associated with youth, or at least with youthful enthusiasm. Now our major sports are professional, and our professionals are very much adult. As Bruce says, there is no way we can hope to change this framework—the arena is too big. It's like trying to change the quality of fast food in the schools by changing the food industry. And the same thing might be said about the chief criticisms of pro football today—violence and rowdiness. Is it easier to change some of the rules or some of the players, or to change society at large? As Bill Russell says, "If a fan is an embarrassment to the human race at the Super Bowl, it's not because he's at the Super Bowl—it's because he's an embarrassment to the human race."

On the occasions when I get back to the University of California for a football game, I find myself marveling at the irrepressible resources of youth. In spite of wars, upheavals in society, our own personal problems of growing up and coping with changes in life, a good old-fashioned college football game is still the same. I keep struggling with St. Paul's famous sentence in his first letter to the Corinthians: "When I was a child, I spoke as a child, I understood as a child, I thought as a child; but when I became a man, I put away childish things." I still want to have that option of going back to "childish" things. I want to relive the spirit of my old self, but of course not the reality. I want to share in what Bruce Stevenson has: the involvement with young minds.

Every now and then the professional football game allows us to become college players again. I can dispense with cheer- leaders attempting to imitate their college counterparts. Or with fans holding up posters in the hope of catching the eye of TV cameras. But give me more of those games like the one in the snow against New England in Mile High Stadium in 1979. Give me all that sloshing around. Give me a pitchout to a halfback who then pulls up short and sails one into the end zone for a touchdown. Even give me a bad break, if it was part of the old college try. Does it take courage to believe in youth? It must, because we all seem so intent on running away from it.

TEN

TO BELIEVE IN GOD

JEFF WELLS

When Jeff Wells was a freshman at Rice University, he entered a half-marathon—13.1 miles—in Dallas along with his roommate, who was a member of the cross-country team. Jeff was just becoming serious about distance running, so shortly after the gun went off he lost his buddy among the five or six leaders, who quickly left the rest of the field behind. It was an out-and-back course along the edge of a lake, which gives the slower runners a chance to see the front-runners after they've made their turn and headed back to the finish. Strangely, Jeff didn't notice his roommate among the leaders as they streaked toward him; perhaps he had an injury and pulled out. But when Jeff finished he couldn't find his friend among the spectators, either. Finally, when the runners had all come in and the crowd was dispersing, his roommate came sprinting toward the finish line as if it was the race of his life. He had fallen behind the leaders and lost sight of them on the winding course, and had completely missed the turnaround and circled the lake! Yet he went on and gave it all he had—without spectators, timers, or other runners around him for company— because, as he told Jeff, the only fan that mattered for him was God. To this day, he says it was his favorite race.

I'm sure it's difficult for most of us to be able to visualize God as a fan. Intellectually, perhaps, we can convince ourselves we are doing something just "for the glory of God," but we are flesh and blood, not pure spirits. We think in terms of sights, sounds, touches. To believe in God means to love Him, yet our only experience of love is of other people, or perhaps pets, or things we can associate with other human feelings, such as fond memories. So we try to recreate God in human terms—with paintings and hymns and ornaments. Unfortunatey, the images we have of God as the old man with the long beard on the throne are hardly lovable, either. Some fan!

Earlier I quoted a beautiful description of this process of "getting to know God," from an essay by Maximus of Tyre in the first century: "But we, being unable to apprehend His essence, use the help of sounds and names and pictures, of beaten gold and ivory and silver, of plants and rivers, mountain peaks and torrents, yearning for the knowledge of Him, and in our weakness naming all that is beautiful in the world after His nature—just as happens to earthly lovers." Unfortunately, it's my experience at any rate that the gold and silver we adorn our churches with are often symbols of our own self-importance rather than love offerings to God. To believe in God to such an extent that one can associate with Him as a friend, a son or daughter, or a fan seems to me to be an awesome challenge. Yet people like Jeff Wells speaks of a love of God as real as a love of a mother for a newborn baby or a man and a woman on their fiftieth wedding anniversary. How does he do it?

A contemporary master storyteller, Isaac Bashevis Singer, recalls an incident from his upbringing in an orthodox Jewish family that says a lot about the problem. At least for his mother, the stories of the Old Testament were quite literal

accounts of God's relationship with the world. But his older
brother was discovering the wonders of the scientific approach
to the world, and one day he challenged his mother's simple
beliefs. "I'm an atheist," he proudly announced; "that story of
creation in the Bible is an unscientific myth." His mother
answered at once, "And, so, who created the universe? You?"

Some people believe in God as the man-with-the-long-
beard-on-the-throne. Their concept of heaven is the cartoon
version: harps, pearly gates, wisps of clouds. Others, who
would call themselves more sophisticated, point out that heaven
can't be "up there" because "up there" is "down there" when
the earth spins 180 degrees. They might believe in a God who
is the "sense of the universe," the God of Spinoza, who is
manifest in everything in the universe—not Nature itself, but
the Spirit that created and continues to infuse nature with its
life. Still others find it difficult to approach the concept of an
almighty, all-knowing God except through the person of Christ.
Among professed believers I'm sure there are many who
believe only by default—it's easier not to bother one's head
too much about it, but hope for the best in some vague
religious way.

Among the athletes I know who have come to some
commitment to the idea of God, most find their strength to
believe in the gospels—in the Lord. Jim Zorn says that people
often open a conversation with him by saying, "Hey, I'm religious, too." But his faith has nothing to do with "religious-
ness," it has to do with the example of Christ. Religiosity is
exemplified in social churchgoing, in dutiful contributions to
the expected church charities, in unthinking acceptance of
church pronouncements—without any daily evidence of the
spirit of Christ in one's life. Some would argue that all these
religious formalities at least do some good in that they keep
reminding us of our faith. It seems to me that the lack of
substance behind them is the sort of hypocrisy that has turned
so many young people away from even the formalities of
religion.

The problem that thinking, concerned persons have with
the notion of God is that *they are afraid man has created God,*
instead of the opposite. Man in his frailty, his weaknesses, his

fear of the future, turns to a hope beyond this troublesome life. He is easily persuaded, some would say duped into believing, that injustice can be suffered in the world because everything will be rectified in the next world. Others would argue that the whole framework of organized religion is, intentionally or not, just a cozy business for "salesmen in the pulpit." Still others see it, on a large scale, as a means of perpetuating class divisions: the opiate of the masses.

A logical, scientific approach to the question might be to settle, once and for all, the question of the existence of God. Then everything else would fall into place—Bible, churches, preaching. Throughout the centuries the world's great thinkers have offered their arguments to "prove the existence of God." But theological arguments, no matter how dressed up in the folds of learning, fail to win men's hearts, let alone change their minds. It would seem to me that if logical arguments were possible, on the order of proving theorems in geometry or demonstrating the solution to a chess problem, then all human beings would have long ago acceded to the fact of God's existence. At the same time, a God who was "provable" by such means wouldn't be much of a God—he would be another theorem. I would prove the existence of the Denver Broncos by showing up in training camp, not by thinking about it. As Tom Landry once said about the difficulty of understanding some of Christ's message, if it were all that simple and easy everybody would have come aboard long ago. But life is never easy and simple.

The nineteenth-century English cardinal, John Newman, wrote in summation of his belief of God: "God's existence is immediately and irrefutably disclosed as soon as we open our eyes to life as it really is." If we want to prove He exists, we should show up in His training camp.

Some time before dawn Jeff Wells is at his desk, reading the Bible. He will spend an hour or so at it, moving through it patiently, a dozen or so pages at a sitting. Then a few minutes of prayer and thought, and he's into his track shoes and off for a five- or six-mile run through the streets of Eugene, Oregon.

He'll spend the rest of the morning in the work of the Calvary Baptist Church there, his current ministry. Then in the afternoon he'll join one of his fellow marathoners, Tony Sandoval or John Lodwick, in a twelve-mile run in the countryside. Two or three times during a month, they'll take off at a race pace— about five minutes per mile—in this afternoon workout. An occasional longer run and some intervals—220-, 330-, and 440-yard sprints interspersed with walking—complete their training program. In late 1979, at the renowned Eugene Marathon, Wells and Sandoval won in a dead heat, with Lodwick not far behind. Their times, all in the two-hour—10-minute range, were three of the best in marathon history. Their goal— to compete for the United States in the 1980 Olympics—went unfulfilled as the Soviet Union invaded Afghanistan.

Jeff has been reading the Bible almost daily ever since the summer before his entry into Rice. He had grown up in what he calls a "semi-Christian" family in the same atmosphere as thousands of other children of the sixties and seventies, yet by his senior year in high school, in Madisonville, Texas, he was attracted to the Christian message in a serious way. Whiling away the summer, he was basking at popular Stewart Beach in Galveston when a rock group came to his attention—only they were playing spiritual music, not hymns or revival songs, but thoughtful music with a Christian message. One fellow in the group stood out in Jeff's mind as the type of person he had confidence in—as others might say, he could relate to him. Jeff knew he had questions to ask, and waited for an opportunity. Ever since they met and talked, says Jeff, God has been the most important part of his life.

At Rice, Jeff continued to play most sports as he had done in high school, as the seasons came up. Basketball was his true love, but he soon realized that his best potential was in long-distance running. His religious focus became so intense that he decided to make a career out of the ministry. He went on to the Dallas Theological Seminary after graduation from Rice, and soon his name began to be mentioned in the same breath with Frank Shorter, the man who made marathoning an American sport with his win at Munich, and with Bill Rodgers, who was his heir apparent. Who was this rugged-faced theology student from Texas who dedicated his races to the Lord?

On Patriots' Day in Boston in 1978, racing conditions were ideal: cool temperatures, even a slight mist, and a field of top competitors. The year before, Rodgers had pulled up with leg cramps after three quarters of the marathon, and walked over to Elliot's Lounge for a beer. People continued to complain about how amateurishly this race was run, but maybe that was part of its charm—it maintained the tradition of amateur sports that brought the most enthusiastic crowds in the world to line its course. The cameras still focused on "Billy White Gloves," because this wraithlike, boyish figure had been building for Boston '78 with impressive wins over the world's best marathoners. As Rodgers crested "Heartbreak Hill" some six miles from the finish, he seemed to be pulling away from the field impressively. Then word reached him that a younger man was moving up through the pack: it was Wells. Rodgers recalls that he began to read the next morning's headlines in his pounding head: "Wells Overtakes Rodgers at Finish." He urged himself on painfully into the last mile as the excitement of the crowd told him the Texan was closing the gap; Boston was his town, his race, and if he didn't make it now he might be crushed forever. Over the last three hundred yards ten or fifteen yards separated the two runners. But the hometown hero was not to be denied, and he plunged through the tape a matter of seconds ahead of Wells. Rodgers has since gone on to dominate both Boston and New York, the two major marathons in the country, but this one—a record—will always be remembered as one of the most exciting races in the history of the sport.

Though the tension of marathon competition was suddenly snapped by the Olympic boycott in 1980, Jeff Wells intends to continue competing for many years, as he enters a full-time ministry. And he knows he will always run. He writes: "Many of us run simply because it is fun. Also, we may run because of the feeling of accomplishment that accompanies finishing a tough workout or race. Some people are attracted to the human drama portrayed in running. Still others are motivated by the camaraderie among runners and the excitement that comes with improvement. Many are motivated to run because it is good for their health. All of these are good reasons for running. But we can also glorify God in our running." He explains that for many of us running is an exercise of our God-given talents. To look for an earthly reward—prizes, recognition, records—demeans the use of that talent. He points to Paul's letter to the Colossians: "Whatever your task, work heartily, as serving the Lord and not man." This is the sense in which God is our fan, our spectator. And this is why competition in football or running or doing one's job can become constructive rather than destructive. For to succeed at someone else's expense is a dead end in the use of one's talents.

Jeff is often asked how his training to be a competitive athlete squares with his Christian ideal of "turning the other cheek" and "doing unto others as you would have them do unto you." They would prefer to "do you in," wouldn't they? He explains that in any competitive sport someone wins and someone loses, but there is a great difference between the attitude of a winner who is striving to do his best and a winner who is merely interested in coming ahead of someone else. Attitude is everything. If competition itself were to be done away with because it always results in winners and losers, then sports would collapse along with every other human striving for excellence. If a shortstop decided not to dive for tough ground balls, because he wanted to relax the competition, he would ruin the game for the other players as well. "If Shorter and Rodgers said to me, 'Look, we'll let you win this one, Jeff,' the race would no longer be of any value for me."

At the Dallas Theological Seminary, Jeff was very much aware of the problem of mixing athletics with religion. One of his professors, Dr. Howard Hendricks, was one of the leaders of the prayer meetings conducted for the Dallas Cowboys. The southwestern United States is a very sports-oriented section of the country; God is constantly being brought into politics or sports as naturally as one would bring in the weather. Jeff points out that contests of one kind or another form the basis of parables and stories in the Bible, the most prominent being Paul's references to "running the good race, fighting the good fight"; Tom Landry draws frequently on these quotations. What it comes down to, in Jeff's view, is giving the glory of the accomplishment to God, but doing the work yourself. He quotes Paul to the Galatians: "God is not mocked. Whatever a man sows, that he will also reap."

A modern equivalent of that sentiment is the answer I've heard to that old pep talk: "We can beat those guys; they're only human. They put their pants on one leg at a time." "Yes, but that's where the similarity ends."

One of Jeff Wells's favorite stories in the Bible—because of the stark moral of the encounter for athletes—is David-Goliath meeting in 1 Samuel (also known as 1 Kings). As Jeff retells it in his booklet on competition, *No Fading Wreath*, this tale has a lot more to it than the lesson that a smaller person can overcome a giant if he has the right weapons. If that's all there was to the story, it would be simply another nice old saw from ancient times—a sort of Aesop's fable. And this example also instructs us in how to read the Bible: not in condensed, picture-book form, but in the full richness of the storyteller's words. As Jeff says, the chapter in which the David-Goliath story appears might well be considered the front page of the sports section of the Bible.

David's father had sent him to the battlefield to bring some bread and cheese to his brothers, who were in King Saul's army. "The army had raised its war cry and gone out to fight; Israel was now marshaled for battle, and the Philistines awaited them. So David left all the gifts he had brought with him in care of the baggage master, and ran to the field of battle, to see how his brothers fared. Even as he spoke, out came the champion of the Philistine cause, Goliath ... and David heard him repeat his customary challenge. All the men of Israel were shrinking away in terror from the sight of him, and the talk went round among them: Have you seen the warrior that went by?" No one dared take up Goliath's challenge to individual combat, but David immediately said he would go out to meet him "to save Israel's honor."

One of David's older brothers happened to be nearby, and overheard David's remark. He "turned upon David in anger: Why have you come here, he asked? Why must your sorry flock go astray in the desert? This is your old self-conceit, your old cunning. You have only come here to watch the battle!" But David insisted he would take on Goliath, and since he was the only one to speak up he was soon brought to the king. Needless to say, Saul was unimpressed by what he saw. "What! You're going to meet the Philistine and engage him in battle? Why, you are only a boy, and this is a man trained in arms from his youth." But David had been to training camp, in spite of what his brothers thought. "My lord, I used to feed my father's flock; and if a lion or bear came and carried off one of my rams, I would go in pursuit, and get the upper hand, and take the prey from their jaws. If they threatened me, I would grab them by the throat and strangle them. . . . The Lord who protected me against lion and bear will protect me against the Philistine."

Saul agreed to let him have a try at Goliath, and gave him his own armor to wear. But it was too cumbersome for David—he was a sort of scatback. So he went out to meet the giant of a man with his staff, his sling, and five stones. Goliath "looked at David with contempt. Here was a boy, red-cheeked and fair of face. What? he said, Do you take me for a dog that you come to meet me with a staff? He cursed David and said, Come here— let me give your carrion to the animals and birds." But David answered with equal effrontery, saying that he would kill Goliath to prove that "God rules the battle—the Lord sends victory without the help of sword or spear."

The outcome of the battle is well known to everyone who has the slightest acquaintance with the Bible. David hit Goliath on the forehead with his first shot from his sling. With their champion dead, the Philistines retreated in dismay. And David was on his way up.

The reason why Jeff Wells tells this story in such detail, and why I've done the same here, is to show how even the familiar scenes in the Bible have a depth of interpretation that makes rereading them consistently enlightening. The story itself isn't the thing: the motivations, the attitudes *are*. There is the concern of the father for his son's welfare in the army; the skepticism and belittling of David's older brother; the faith of the king; the contempt of Goliath; the self-confidence and preparation of David, and his trust in God at the same time; and above all his motivation. As the story continues, jealousy starts to gnaw at Saul as the women come out to sing about David's triumph: "By Saul's hand a thousand, by David's ten thousand fell." A businessman, a father or mother, a struggling student, a rejected athlete, or a Super Bowl champion can all profit from the inherent message in stories like this. But the message is between the lines, and makes its impact only after consistent reading and rereading of large portions of both the Old and New Testament. Our minds are worn smooth by the regular, year-in, year-out rubbing against the judgments and decisions we see in these dynamic stories. As Newman comments:

> One of the most remarkable characteristics of Scrip-ture narrative ... is the absence of expressions by which the reader can judge whether the events re-corded are presented for praise or blame. A plain, bare series of facts is drawn out; and whether they are for imitation or warning often cannot be decided ex-cept by the context, or by the event, or by our general notions of propriety.

I have no doubt that Jeff Wells is what he is today because of that habit he acquired in that summer before college—of spending some time each day reading "the Good Book."

The idea of facing the mystery of God is not very fashion-able these days. But running a marathon used to be considered an impossible ordeal; now it has become a hobby of many middle-aged men. Jeff Wells shies away from the idea that long-distance running is a form of meditation for him, or that it produces a mental equilibrium akin to transcendental medi-tation. Running simply relaxes him, enables him to observe "God's handiwork, the outdoors." In a race, he goes through the same anxieties and self-doubts about his ability to push himself to the limits of his endurance; but this is the only place in which God might enter into his avocation. As soon as he reassures himself that he is running for God's glory, his fears abate. He has that degree of communication with God only because he has done his training with God, too. He puts in, per week, more than 100 miles in the pursuit of God as well as in the pursuit of Rodgers.

Jeff's communication with his God doesn't come from insights that leap off the pages of his reading, or from visions he experiences while praying—though all of that helps. The communication is in his own heart. Again, Cardinal Newman makes his point:

> *It is a deceit and a mischief to think to understand the Christian doctrines as a matter of course merely by being taught by books, or by attending sermons, or by any outward means, however excellent, taken by themselves. For it is in proportion as we search our hearts and understand our own nature that we understand what is meant by an Infinite Governor and Judge. . . . God speaks to us primarily in our own hearts. Self-knowledge is the key to the precepts and doctrines of the scriptures. The very utmost any outward notices of religion can do is to startle us and make us turn inward and search our hearts; and then, when we have experienced what it is to read ourselves, we shall profit by the doctrines of the Church and the Bible.*

The great hope of the churches, condemned though they may have been by a secular society on the one hand and by iconoclastic rebels on the other, is that they will have leaders like Jeff Wells who look for the substance of religion in the heart instead of in cathedrals. A fellow Baptist and fellow Texan, Buckner Fanning, has shown some remarkable new directions the churches might take to bring this about. Curiously, Wells and Fanning also share a role in the running movement.

In 1945, a detachment of U.S. Marines was sent in to Hiroshima after Japan's surrender to assess the damage of the world's first nuclear bombing and to take charge of the evacuation and restoration of that grim locale. Fanning was among them, and what he saw there changed him from a devil-may-care Marine into a dedicated emissary of God. On leaving the service, Fanning enrolled at a Baptist seminary and went on to the ministry. In time, he was able to take his message around the world as a preacher in various foreign Baptist congregations—including Japan and countries behind the Iron Curtain. He discovered that the countries of the Soviet bloc really didn't restrict religious worship, but religious freedom. In other words, the faithful were allowed to attend their churches, but they were forbidden to preach outside them. Thus, Fanning was told in Hungary that he could hold the Bible, but not read from it, and he could visit with the congregation, but not give a sermon from the pulpit. All right; he decided to give his sermon by walking up and down the aisles of the church, simply conversing with the people. The reaction was instantaneous: he never felt closer to the real message of the gospel.

On his return to San Antonio, his home, he decided to try the same experiment on his own congregation—the Trinity Baptist Church. He removed the imposing pulpit and delivered his thoughts walking up and down the aisles. At first the reaction was disquieting—after so many years of the accustomed way of doing things, the members of the congregation felt cheated. They wanted their minister up there on a pedestal, just as they kept putting Christ up on a pedestal instead of trying to understand Him as a human being, just like them. But gradually the experiment took hold. Perhaps the pulpits will now be coming down in many other churches.

It was in one of Fanning's congregations, incidentally, that he was treated by a young doctor for injuries received in a serious automobile accident. While recuperating, Fanning felt the need for some form of exercise to build up his stamina— some measurable system that would allow him to regain his health without danger. The doctor was Kenneth Cooper; the formula was aerobics. And thus was born, with assists from Coach Bill Bowerman at the University of Oregon in Eugene, among a few others, the running movement.

Jeff Wells's experience in getting Christ down out of the pulpit has come not only from his intense involvement in the popular field of distance running, but also from role models he has known through books. One of his favorite books, he says, is the story of a young man who chose as his career to go to the missions in South America: *Shadow of the Almighty,* by that young man's widow, Elizabeth Elliot. In 1956 Jim Elliot was killed by the Indians he was attempting to reach, in Ecuador. Jim's great heart was obviously a heart he had searched for communication with God. Another strong influence in Jeff's thinking has been the British theologian, J. I. Packer, whose *Knowing God* is a modern attempt to confront the Almighty, without the symbols that have tended to make the God of tradition a formidable and fearsome Being.

Above everything else, Jeff's alliance with God is a joyful, exuberant thing to see. Bill Russell says, "Ask me a thousand different questions about religion and I'll say only that I believe there's something going on out there that fills me with joy and wonder." There's something going on in this lanky Texan that also fills me with joy and wonder. God is in him. If his mother happened to ask, "And, so, who created the universe? You?" his answer might be a partial yes.

ELEVEN

TO BELIEVE IN LIFE

JIM ZORN

It was only an exhibition game, but Coach Landry doesn't like to be down 31–14. It was time to save Roger Staubach or Clint Longley for better days. Landry turned to the man behind him and said, "Zorn, warm up—you're going in."

"WHAT?" came the reply.

"You're going in—start warming up," somebody else yelled. The next few minutes were a blur in Jim Zorn's mind. His helmet was on, his heart was pounding, and suddenly he was on the field. A play came in with a guard, but for the life of him Zorn couldn't remember the formation. "So I'd call the play, and we'd run up to the line of scrimmage and then I'd try to figure out what I was going to do—right there at the line of scrimmage at the last second." And so it went play after play—only things began to work. There were a few first downs, then one big play and they had driven eighty yards for a touchdown. "It was unbelievable! I was going nuts. I couldn't believe I'd done it. But I can still remember my stats. I was six for ten for sixty-six yards, and I scrambled twice for fourteen. It was a blast!"

That was 1975, but the dream of playing for Dallas, as we shall see, faded. A year later, Jerry Rhome observed a young man at a quarterback school he was conducting. "I thought this kid was like a young deer who came out of the woods with springs in his arms and legs, all full of life. Jim Zorn looked as if he could stand there and jump eighteen feet in the air. He was wild, and nobody had corralled him. That first afternoon I laid eyes on him, I thought, 'This is it!' Jerry Rhome happens to be the quarterback-receiver coach of the Seattle Seahawks, and that year, 1976, he transformed Jim Zorn from a floundering learner into an outstanding rookie quarterback for the just-born Seattle team.

Unlike most of the quarterbacks I know in this game, Zorn somehow managed to keep a kid's enthusiasm alive through college, through the break-in period, through the flush of his initial success. In four short years he has grown to become the terror of the league, as I and Ken Stabler and Steve Bartkowski have come to learn from first-hand experience. Interestingly, for the focus of this book, he has also shown us another side of the younger generation—for he's only in his mid-twenties and he's been a committed Christian since his high school days.

Let's go back a bit—to that idea of a football player most of us have, if he's regularly seen in headlines on sports pages. You know the routine: outstanding high schooler, scholarship to USC or Cal or Ohio State or Syracuse, chance at the Heisman Trophy, top draft choice, big contract, understudy to a famous NFL quarterback or running back, triumph in the Super Bowl. The last is yet to come, of course, for Jim Zorn, but the truth is that none of the other items apply, either. Jim worked hard at Gahr High in Cerritos, California, but he wasn't even a starter until his senior year. There were no inducements, no scholarships to college. Jim paid his way to Cerritos College, where he studied, played a limited form of football, and began to form friendships with kids who attended Bible classes. Yes, he was taking his commitment to life seriously even at that uncertain age.

Zorn made no impression here, either, so he enrolled at California Polytechnic at Pomona. Cal Poly is in a sort of minor league of what was then the "Pac Eight." Jim reached his full height of six feet two inches there, and began to click. In his senior year, he started to make headlines and receive awards: he was "Little All Coast," meaning he made the all-star team of the minor Pacific Coast league. With the yards he had run up or passed for, he stood out with the pro scouts—or so he thought. The NCAA had heard of him, because he was a "player of the week" once during the season.

The pro draft came with great expectations. Jim watched the reports as the first eight rounds were completed: he wasn't among the chosen. There would be a complete result the following morning, so Jim went to bed with limited expectations. He thought about how it would feel to move to an eastern city, or about where the fans would be the best. He picked up a copy of the next day's afternoon paper, and searched the list of 288 college kids who had been drafted. But he couldn't find his name! "I couldn't believe it. I read the list over and over to make sure. Hey—what is this? Didn't I lead the nation in total offense last year? What's with those guys? God, what are you trying to tell me?" Throughout that day, the blackest in his young life, Jim heard the condolences and the reservations of friends. What happened? What about those stats? "My swelled head shrunk to the size of a prune." But this was not to be, by any means, the hardest day of his attempt at a pro football career.

What does a young man do when he's finished his college days, has a national reputation, and isn't wanted by the pros? With twenty-four teams making twelve picks each, that's 288 college players who beat him out. He can go back to school and forget football; he can get a job and play semi-pro to keep his hand in the game; or he can try to catch on as a free agent. Jim was too intent on making it in the NFL to do anything but the latter. After some inquiries with scouts, he was able to sign on for a tryout with the Dallas Cowboys. Picture the scene: a gymnasium with about 125 husky young men jostling each other, trying to size up the twelve lucky ones who are there as draftees, comparing biceps and height and college letters. The first day there's a basic workout for each category: offensive linemen, defense, running backs, and quarterbacks. By night-fall at least twenty-five men are dismissed. The survivors are given an orientation talk the next morning by Coach Landry, who passes briefly over his own philosophy of the game, his personal faith, and his advice to newcomers: "There'll be a lot of bitterness and anger on the practice fields as various team-mates get cut, but this is a contest between you and yourself. It's not the end of the world if you don't make the team. Just do your best and walk away satisfied, regardless of the outcome."

Staubach and Longley were there, too—the number one and two quarterbacks on the team—to pass along their exper-tise on the Dallas offense. Eight newcomers were vying for the coveted third spot, and a month of drills and scrimmages and intrasquad games lay ahead to test their mettle. The physical pressure soon soaks up jealousies and fears; even a well-conditioned twenty-one-year-old like Zorn could only collapse each night from exhaustion. Although he was not yet passing with accuracy, Jim impressed the coaches with his zest. They also had to laugh that, like the young Staubach, he was eager to scramble and could take pressure from charging linemen without losing his concentration. To his amazement, he won the number three job, and joined the forty-three-man team as it prepared for preseason games. He credited Staubach with turning him into a pro:

> *He taught me how to be competitive. He'd be racing me*
> *in the drills. He didn't have to race me—I was no*
> *threat to him. But he just did it. That's Roger.*

There was some talk around camp that summer that Dallas could use another running back. Two days before the first pre-season game, the veteran Preston Pearson was put on waivers by Pittsburgh. Dallas snapped him up. Now they had to make room for him among the forty-three men that's the league limit. Landry called Jim into his office and began a painful explanation: two of their running backs had been injured and they needed Pearson. They would have to do without a third quarterback. "You can make it in the pros," Landry assured him, "and you deserve to be on this team. I'm sorry to have to let you go."

Zorn crammed his clothes into his suitcase and headed home to Los Angeles to face the second round of humiliation and defeat that year. "That was the hardest day of my life so far, right there," he says. "Then I examined myself—what did I want? Pride? Respect? Fame? Deep inside me, I knew I had to praise God for what happened. I had to accept it as part of His plan for me. It wasn't the end of the world—even though I thought I might never play football again." There was still a chance to catch on with the Rams—and they gave him a quick tryout. At the time they felt secure with two quarterbacks, James Harris and Ron Jaworski, but they had a hankering for Zorn, too. They suggested that he practice with the team but stay out of sight—officially. They would keep him on the payroll and in reserve for the following year—"stashing," it's called. When Jim was told of the full implications of this sort of league infraction, he once again walked away from the playing field. The only NFL football he saw that year was on his parents' TV set.

The twenty-two-year-old would-be quarterback kept in shape throughout the winter and headed for Seattle the following spring to see if he could find a place with the fledgling Seahawks. He heard they had a free-wheeling coach named Jack Patera and a team that had nowhere to go but up. That's when Jerry Rhome laid eyes on him, and since then the Seahawks have jumped eighteen feet in the air.

The headquarters of the Seattle Seahawks hovers over the eastern shore of Lake Washington in a little community called Kirkland, across the water from Seattle. Ray Guy could punt one into the sailboats from the emerald-green practice field next to the Seahawks' office, which resembles mostly a spiffy yacht club. Considering the frustrations the Oakland Raiders once experienced at the hands of Seattle, he might well want to.

It's early January, 1980. The only football stories in the

papers are focused on the Super Bowl, but life goes on as usual at a professional football organization. The Seahawks, with 9–7 records the last two years, are sold out for 1981; the problem is to find an equitable way to deal with requests for tickets—they decide to hold a block of general admission tickets open before each game. In the publicity office, the official stats for the previous season are being cranked out and disseminated. Special events are being planned, such as the Gold Helmet Awards, in which Patera was named the NFL coach of the year and Terry Bradshaw the NFL player of the year, for 1978. There is speculation about who might be the Seahawks' MVP. Down the hall, coaches and scouts are reviewing the draft scene, some three months away. In an office of his own, Jim Zorn is writing letters to friends in the league, answering fan mail, getting ready to take a turn in the weight room, or to play some racquetball. A very pregnant young lady, with a farm-fresh smile and jokes in her eyes, pops in to ask about lunch.

"Meet my wife Joy," Jim says. "She works here, too." They've been married since April, and are starting right in on a family. They live on an island across from downtown Seattle, raise roses and a few fruit trees in their backyard. The latter fact inspired a sportswriter to lament, "What! The Raiders knocked out of the playoffs by a rose gardener?"

On a salary unseasonably large for a typical young couple—good NFL quarterbacks are expected to make in excess of $200,000 a year—the Zorns manage to live close to the earth and to their backgrounds. Until last year, their car was an older Volkswagen whose odometer had gone around twice, and they still pride themselves on being comparison shoppers. "I always wanted a Porsche," Jim admits, "but now I don't know if I care that much. Other things have come into our lives." They share a basic Christian outlook and are especially interested in doing something for young people. "We're not preachers. What we're saying to the kids is that there's an alternative: you don't have to grow up to be a 'street person.' "

Jim traces his early involvement in Christian action back to a "Youth for Christ" session he once attended in high school. He was dragged along by a girlfriend whom he was trying to win back, but he soon was hooked on the presentation that a teacher, Don Hildebrand, made about the Bible. He maintained this interest in college, attending the "Insight" programs offered there. "It was more compelling than any kind of drug," he says; "my eyes were really opened to Christ. He was always just a symbol to me, but now He became real."

The dashing young hero of the Seahawks fluttered many a heart in those first few years of professional action. But it was a chance meeting in a coffee shop that brought Jim and Joy together. She was a waitress, working her work through the University of Washington; he asked for a date, which turned into a four-hour conversation about morality, religion, modern families, and the Equal Rights Amendment. In her sociology classes she took exception to the anything-goes attitude of her professors, as if ethics was irrelevant in human relations. The idea that only consequences had to be calculated in a decision, not morality, left her cold. She also was put off by Jim's "typical male approach," for he was accustomed to opening doors and standing back in elevators for women. She wanted to be treated as a complete equal. For his part Jim was taken aback, for all through college and his early pro career he thought he was "pretty cool," he knew how women thought. Within two years they were married and working together in youth guidance programs.

A young man in Levi's and T-shirt wanders in, sporting a cast on his wrist. Steve Largent broke it in the first quarter of the second Denver game—the first time they ever beat the Broncos. Then, with a couple of minutes to go, he came back in, caught a Zorn bomb, and took the game away from us as if we were trying to make room for the handicapped. "Hey Steve," Jim confirms, "you guys are coming over for hamburgers tonight, right?" Ron Koder, another outstanding Seahawk, pokes his head in the door: "How about me?" Ron's bushy, pitchblack beard makes him look a little senior to the others, but without the shoulder pads and helmets they might all appear to have just walked off the Washington campus. "What do you think of that swimming pool deal?" Steve asks. "You mean all we have to do is stand in their booth and they'll give us one?" They have entered the world of endorsements.

In 1922 an unheralded writer/poet produced a little volume entitled *Ceremonials of Common Days*. To columnist Dannye Romine we owe the rediscovery of Abbie Graham, who believes in life so mightily she celebrates it in its little things, its daily occurrences, its backyard roses and patio barbecues. She doesn't spell it with a capital "L" and she doesn't draw lessons in morality from its events. But she *believes* in it:

> *Of Celestial Shopping: Easter Day is my day for the collection of the beauty of all transitory things. This is the Season of the Relinquishment of Things, and it is, therefore, the time for an intensified appreciation of them. The list below of the things I would like to take to heaven with me is quite incomplete, for I have not yet had leisure to love everything.*
>
> *One Tea-room, serving cinnamon toast by a fire-place. . . . One Head Waiter with one Sub-waiter. A small garden. A stony brook. A small post office.*

Her list goes on, challenging us to see the exquisiteness of creation in the ordinary. Yet it is a catalog of values uniquely human, as much as for the fact that they are transitory as that they mirror the precious gift of sight, sound, touch, and thought that we possess so thanklessly. She asks us to exclaim, "What a blast!"

There are little treasures in the bruising game of football, as much as there are giant things—like upsets and wins and crushing defeats—that wilt even faster. I especially like Jim Zorn's description of the frustration of the men who are paid to chase him around the backfield:

> *Oh, I'll never forget our first year. The Seahawks were playing Atlanta in the Kingdome, and there was an Atlanta man named Claude Humphrey—a big strong sucker—who was getting frustrated because every time I'd pass he'd knock me down just a split second after I'd release it. He'd get so mad because he thought he'd tackled me with the ball, but then the ball would be gone. I'll tell you he was a great guy, and he was really having a blast because his motivation for the game was to nail me with that ball. Finally, he came*

back inside on one play before I saw him and just laid into me. That time he just knew I hadn't gotten rid of the ball. Man, he started yelling and hooting and having the greatest time, and about four times he said, "I GOT YA, ZORN, I GOT YA!"

Jim also describes things that go on in a huddle that I guess everyone in the game knows about but never thinks worth mentioning. During time-outs, for example, a huddle will be broken up into various conversations: linemen will discuss what's going on with the defense, receivers will talk with each other about patterns, and someone will chime in with a pep talk. The quarterback tries to take it all in. But when a drive is under way, you'll see the quarterback stand outside the huddle for a few seconds—he doesn't want to lose his concentration, even though he usually isn't calling the plays. Let's say Patera then sends in a play. As soon as the runner arrives at the huddle, the conversations stop and the quarterback joins in. As Jim says, "Now they're talking on my time and I only have thirty seconds to call the play, get up to the line, and possibly have an audible. So I make eye contact with the guys involved—you can't call a play looking down at the ground—because you want to look at them with confidence, as if the play is going to *work*. You want to project that confidence in your voice. I usually call the play just once, and then it's up to the line."

If the coach sends in all the plays, as do Landry and Miller and everybody but Noll and a few others, then what's the point of an audible? Actually, the quarterback has a very limited sequence of things he can do to *replace* the coach's call by an audible at the line. So the coach may see a different pattern than what he called, but he won't see a trap play when he wants a pitchout.

Quarterbacks are often asked about violence in the pro game, with the implication that there's something unhealthy in American life if we thrill to injuries and fights and vendettas in our sports. In his first year with Seattle, Zorn was sacked twenty-eight times—among them that mighty spill in Atlanta. He was out briefly with a sprained ankle and a face fracture. Lately he's been more careful, by not being so eager to run.

Other players have been severely injured, and the risks are great for receivers and running backs. But with good conditioning a player in pro football is safer than a skier, or a driver without a seat belt. But why argue about relative risks? The whole argument about physical injuries and violence ignores the other extreme: doing nothing, ignoring life, letting it pass us by without a blink. I've said enough about the hazards of the game, things all of us would like to change. It takes a person like Jim Zorn to show us what there is to relish in life when we approach it with youthful innocence. As Christ said, "I came to bring life, and life more abundantly."

The game that showed me this side of James Arthur Zorn more than anything else was their 1979 31–28 win over Atlanta. In it Jack Patera invented a new phrase for the sportscasters to kick around: the fourth-down conversion. Did you ever notice the unsophisticated fan at a college game, who's always shouting "Go for it!"? It may be fourth down. His team may be on their own twenty-yard line with seven to go for a first down. The fans around him smile indulgently at that shout, "Go for it!" But consider this: In the latter part of the third quarter, the Seahawks held a 24–14 lead. After three plays from their thirty-four they managed to lose two yards, facing a fourth and twelve. The Atlanta fans roared a cheer for the defense, and their punt-return team went on the field. Seattle was appearing on a regular-season national telecast for the first time, struggling to improve its 3–5 record. Patera sent in a pass play! And it was complete, but the receiver was dragged down after only a nine-yard gain. But the other three times the Seahawks "went for it" on fourth down, the result was a touchdown. First Zorn ran it in himself from thirty-four yards out, then he took the pass from center for a field-goal attempt, stood up, and fired a twenty-yard pass to the place kicker, Efren Herrera, to keep the drive going. What are they trying to do up there in the Northwest, change this back into a boys' game? The last time I saw this happen was when Oregon State did it in the Rose Bowl a few years back.

And I'll tell you what takes courage: not just to "play hurt" or to go for the extra yard with your face mask, or to keep your eye on a receiver when a blitz is on. The real test is psychological—to believe in the gift of *life* when things start falling apart all around you. That one game that Jim Zorn played in the exhibition season as a Cowboy was against the Oakland Raiders. (It was the first time, by the way, that three left-handed quarterbacks, Dave Humm and Ken Stabler as well as Zorn, played in a pro game together. There's some trivia for you.) He engineered that eighty-yard drive against one of the best defensive units in the game, making the score respectable in the loss: 31–21. Since then he's been a killer against Oakland. But in a more recent appearance, the final game of the 1979 season, the mental pressure was really on. The Oakland crowd thundered a welcome to the Raiders at the Coliseum, for they had fought their way back from a seemingly hopeless midseason record to have a chance at the playoffs. The previous week, Seattle and Zorn and Largent had derailed our big orange train, and we would have to fight for our lives for the division championship in a Monday-night football game at San Diego. All Oakland had to do was win one, at long last, from the 8–7 Seahawks, and then watch *us* under pressure against the red-hot Chargers.

Oakland kicked off and Zorn and company took over at the twenty. On second down he went into the flat with a side-line pattern, and overthrew. The ball was tipped into the hands of the Raider cornerback, who sprinted in for the score. In a matter of seconds, the Seahawks had spotted the Raiders seven points. I've seen momentum like that built up to a rout in Oakland; we did it to New England in the snow in Denver earlier that year. But the Seahawks went back out onto the field, started throwing just as confidently, and took the Raiders apart. You might say the Broncos and I had a special interest in that game, because of the playoff berth it guaranteed us. But I was fascinated more by the "comeback" strength it showed in a young and enthusiastic bunch of players. For earlier in the season, as I recounted in chapter one, we had demoralized them with our own impossible comeback. And just when they were regaining their feet the Rams came along and kocked them back with a *minus* offensive yardage at the Kingdome. That's football, and, even more intensely, that's life. And *life* is what Christ's message is all about.

To see life for what it is, I think you've got to become
unsophisticated, forget about the odds, take each moment as a
new window on the world and little things as important as
anything else. A fellow named Peter Jenkins tried to do something like this to rediscover America. He quit his job and
began a walk across the country that would take him five years.
As he describes this adventure in *A Walk Across America,* I see
something of the freshness of youth, the joy of life that is Jim
Zorn's. In Mobile, Alabama, he encountered not only a city that
astonished him with its foliage ("a city where man and nature
existed in harmony"), but a religious experience others might
laugh at. On his way to a party, he was confronted with a bill-
board announcing an old-fashioned religious revival. It was
James Robison, a man he had never heard of but who has
influenced thousands with his dynamic performances. Out of
curiosity, out of his avowed goal of looking into everything
American, he decided to go. There were the usual hymns, and
then a man "rushed to the microphone like a Dallas Cowboy."
It was Robison, Jenkins recounts:

> *I didn't really believe all this nonsense about eternity,
> but I was more interested than I wanted to admit. . . .
> Most of what he said, about knowing God, repenting,
> and salvation I didn't clearly understand. . . . Some-
> thing about this whole scene made me nervous and
> uncomfortable. As unexpected as death, embarrassing
> tears began to roll down my face. A gentle hand was
> wiping away something inside of me.*

Robison's persuasive, explosive, perceptive presentation,
modulated like the rise and fall of the sea, had washed into his
consciousness. It was like that sudden calmness that came
over Tom Landry in a Bible discussion, or that complete resig-
nation that Terry Bradshaw made in the privacy of his apartment, or that anguished cry that Jim Ryun made at Munich, or
Jim Zorn's opening of his eyes in that college Insight group.
Jenkins describes it lyrically: "It still seemed too simple. But I
felt clearer, cleaner, and different than ever before in my
life. . . . Now I knew what people meant when they sang
'Amazing Grace'."

Do you have the courage to believe these well-worn lines? They are the challenge as well as the strength in every Christian life. For Christ came to give us life, and life more abundantly.

> *Therefore, I tell you, do not be anxious about your life, what you shall eat or what you shall drink, or about your body, what you shall put on. Is not life more than food and body more than clothing? . . . Ask, and it will be given; seek and you shall find; knock and the door will be opened.*